A Bedouin Century

with best wishes
عارف ابو ربیعه
Nov. 10, 2003

A Bedouin Century

*Education and Development among the
Negev Tribes in the 20ᵗʰ Century*

Dr. 'Aref Abu-Rabi'a

Berghahn Books
New York • Oxford

First published in 2001 by

Berghahn Books

www.berghahnbooks.com

Library of Congress Cataloging-in-Publication Data

Abu-Rabia, Aref.
    A Bedouin century : education and development among the Negev tribes in the 20th
century / 'Aref Abu-Rabi'ah
        p. cm.
    Includes bibliographical references (p.) and index.
    ISBN 1-57181-832-4 (cl. : alk. paper)
        1. Bedouins--Education--Israel--Negev--History--20th century. 2.
Education--Israel--Negev--History--20th century. 3. Negev (Israel)--Social
conditions--20th century. I. Title.

LA1444.N44 A38 2001
370'.95694'9--dc21   2001043958

British Library Cataloguing in Publication Data

A catalogue record for this book is available from the British Library.

Printed in the United States on acid-free paper.

Contents

Abbreviations

Encyc. Palest.	Encyclopaedia Palaestina. (Beirut).
IDF	Israeli Defense Forces. *The Negev Bedouin in Israel*, 1954.
ISA	Israel State Archives.
P.E.I.	*Personalities in Eretz-Israel 1799–1948, A Biographical Dictionary.*
D.N.B.	The Dictionary of National Biography.
D.N.B.1931-1940	*The Dictionary of National Biography*, edited by L.G. Wickham Legg. London: Oxford University Press, 1949.
D.N.B. 1941-1950	The Dictionary of National Biography, edited by L. G. Wickham Legg and E.T. Williams. London: Oxford University Press, 1959.
D.N.B. 1951-1960	The Dictionary of National Biography, edited by E.T. Williams and Helen M. Palmer. London: Oxford University Press, 1971.
D.N.B. 1961-1970	The Dictionary of National Biography, edited by E.T. Williams and C.S. Nicholls. Oxford: Oxford University Press, 1981.
FO	Foreign Office (Britain)
PRO	Public Record Office, London.
Statis.Abst.Palst.	Statisticals Abstracts of Palestine.
STR	Sterling, a British Pound.

Preface

*I*n this book, I have set out to present a snapshot of the Bedouin in the Negev region in the twentieth century, from the standpoint of education and development; comparing them with the Bedouin in Arab countries.

I have used a descriptive approach to survey the development of the Bedouin. Special emphasis is given to education, to the impact it has had on the Bedouin, and the effect it has had in changing them from nomads to an almost sedentary population, from illiterates to educated people.

One of the things that influenced my decision to write this book has been my work over twenty-five years in the educational system amongst the Bedouin tribes in the Negev: as a teacher; as head of the Bedouin Teachers Training Department at Kaye Teachers College, Beersheba; as an inspector; and finally, as the official in charge of Bedouin education in the Negev District of the Israel Ministry of Education and Culture.

At the age of seventeen and a half, I began to work as an elementary school teacher, I must admit, without qualifications except for a matriculation certificate. There was simply a shortage of teachers in the Bedouin sector. While teaching, I completed my teacher's training and then studied education and Hebrew literature at Ben-Gurion University of the Negev. I went on to graduate school, earning a master's degree in public health, at the Hadassah Medical School in Jerusalem, and then a Ph.D. in anthropology, at Tel-Aviv University. All during those years, I continued to teach, except for two years studying anthropology at the University of London, after completion of my master's degree. After completion of my doctorate at Tel-Aviv University, I received a two-year post-doctoral fellowship at Ben-Gurion University. During those two years, I decided, for personal reasons, to leave the Ministry of Education and devote myself to teaching and research at the university. I reached a final decision in the matter only after I promised myself to document the development of the educational system amongst the Negev Bedouin in the twentieth century, from my own perspective.

This book comprises seven chapters. In Chapter One, I endeavor to provide a survey of the history of the Negev Bedouin, with emphasis on the Ottoman period and the early twentieth century. In this chapter, I deal with the founding of the first Bedouin city—Beersheba—and its becoming a centre of settlement, education, public services and administration, and the seat of the *qaimaqam*s of the Negev District. This chapter also examines how the process of settlements and education affected the Bedouin tribes in the Negev and describes various factors that contributed to developing a new educated Bedouin leadership and creating internal as well as external tribal relationships.

Chapter Two comprises a survey of the establishment and development of an educational system in Beersheba, and the impact it had on the Negev Bedouin, especially on the sons of sheikhs and notables. It also deals with the impact of the First World War on the lives of the Bedouin and the conclusion of the Ottoman period in 1917.

Chapter Three deals with the beginning of the period of the British mandatory regime, which lasted from 1917 to 1948. This chapter expands upon the mandatory period in Palestine in the context of settlement, employment, and such services as the police and health. Also treated in Chapter Three is the web of relations that took root between the Bedouin and British.

Chapter Four describes the impact of the British period on the Bedouin from the standpoint of the creation of a stratum of educated Bedouin leaders, consisting of the sons of sheikhs and notables. The educational systems in Beersheba and the Bedouin tribes in the Negev are described. The chapter deals with the impact of World War II on the Bedouin of the Negev and the Middle East in general, and concludes with the termination of the British period and the establishment of the State of Israel.

Chapter Five deals with the educational system amongst the Negev Bedouin in Israel from 1948 to 1998. The development of the educational system and its institutions is traced, and figures are given for the student population, number of teachers, and elementary and secondary schools in operation over the years.

Chapter Six surveys and provides a detailed list of the clans and tribes of the Negev Bedouin, and the tribal sheikhs. It furthermore provides biographical sketches of a number of outstanding figures among the educated tribal leaders, from the beginning of the century to the present, and their influence on members of their tribes.

In Chapter Seven, I have endeavored, in all due modesty, to survey educational services amongst the Bedouin throughout the Middle East, relying on published sources as well as interviews with Bedouin in the Sinai, Egypt, and Jordan.

This book is based on first and secondary sources, interviews with key people, and archival and documentary material I collected during my work with the Ministry of Education and Culture, as well as research I conducted over the five consecutive years from 1993 to 1998.

My research was supported by a grant from the British Council in Tel-Aviv and the Department of Middle East Studies at the Ben-Gurion University of the Negev, to both of which I owe a debt of gratitude.

I wish to express special thanks to the staffs of the following archives: Israel State Archives, Jerusalem; Public Record Office, London; British Library Museum.

Special thanks are due as well to the Bedouin, who spared no effort in extending their help to me in preparing this work.

This book is dedicated to my people, the Bedouin of the Middle East.

Chapter 1

Introduction

The term Bedouin is derived from the Arabic word for desert, *badia*; that is, a Bedouin is a desert dweller. The Bedouin are Arabs by nationality, Muslims by religion, belong to the Semitic race, and are descendants of Ishmael and Abraham. The Bedouin have become familiar with the desert over thousands of years.

Many researchers have set out to study the history of the Negev Bedouin, and found themselves confronting several formidable questions:

- Do the Bedouin originate from a single geographic area?
- Do they originate from a single genealogical source?
- Did all the Bedouin come to the Negev during a single period, and if so, when?

Researchers have been aware of several reasons, direct and indirect, for the migration of Bedouin from region to region. The search for grazing ground and water for camels and livestock has always been an essential reason for migration. Migration for this reason has often been attended by wars. Blood feuds are another cause. Traditional Bedouin law requires that when one Bedouin kills another, the relatives of the killer move to a distant place, or else obtain the protection of another tribe. A third source of migration was the spread of Islam in the seventh century. The Islamic armies had comprised Bedouin who came to Palestine with their families and belongings (Abu-Rabi'a 1994: 15-17).

Al-'Aref (1934: 9-34, 231-37) claims that Bedouin tribes have inhabited the Negev for thousands of years. There were Bedouin migrations into the Negev from time immemorial. Sharon (1975: 11-30) tells of three known Bedouin migrations in the desert regions around Palestine in the last 1300 years. The first Bedouin was with the rise of Islam in the seventh century. The armies of the new religion were composed entirely of Bedouin warriors, who came to Syria and Palestine with their families, tents, and flocks.

The second Bedouin migration occurred in the ninth century. This was the migration of two tribes, the Banu Helal and Banu Sulaym, who suddenly burst northwards from the Najd Heights, pushing aside many other tribes, some of which had also invaded the country. The Banu Helal and Banu Sulaym entered the heart of the Sinai Desert via the Jordan Valley and quickly moved on, finally reaching Upper Egypt in the tenth century. Their wandering in Egypt and North Africa continued into the eleventh century.

The attempts of the Fatimids to block the Bedouin resulted in an open revolt against the authorities. In 1013, the Bedouin inaugurated a khalif of their own, as a challenge to the khalif in Cairo. In 1024 they once again rebelled and ruled over a great part of Palestine for the following five years.

The Mamelukes, who ruled Palestine and Syria from the middle of the thirteenth century, had concentrated most of their efforts to control Egypt, particularly Cairo. This Mameluke preoccupation led to the incursion of additional Bedouin tribes into Palestine, where they then established themselves. Of overriding interest to the Mamelukes was the protection of caravans on the main highway between Damascus and Cairo, as well as of pilgrims on their way to Mecca. By the late fifteenth century, which was also towards the end of Mameluke rule, the power of the Bedouin in the country had been such that they were able to paralyse commercial convoys and the flow of pilgrims to Mecca.

The Mameluke authorities, and after them the Ottomans, paid annual sums to the Bedouin sheikhs who lived astride the Hajj highway to ensure that pilgrims on their way to Mecca would not be molested. During the Ottoman period, such payments, called *Surra*, 'bundle', came from the government coffers. This annual payment was made by the *amir al-hajj*, commander of the pilgrimage. Despite these, the Bedouin would always find some pretext or other to attack Hajj convoys. The most famous such assault occurred in

1757, on a convoy which an Ottoman royal wife was traveling. The assault, not far from Karakh, involved many deaths, not least from hunger and thirst in the desert after victims were left destitute by the brigands; few of those who had set out were lucky enough to return to Damascus.

The third Bedouin migration commenced early in the sixteenth century and reached its height in the seventeenth. An upheaval took place within the Shammar tribe, which roamed the region north of Najd in the vicinity of two hills known as Jabal Tay and Jabal Shammar. As large segments of the Shammar wandered northwards, they displaced the previous overlords of the Syrian Desert, the Mawali tribes. According to Jabbur (1995: 514-16), it seems that the Mawalis were among the earliest Bedouin in northern Syria, and that in the early seventeenth century, Shammar tribes began to come from Najd and clash with the Mawali tribes already in the north. Afterwards, the tribes of 'Aniza came from Najd and began to exert pressure on the Mawali tribes with the aim of driving them out of the regions near Hems and Hamah, the most productive agricultural and pasture lands, with plentiful rainfall. It seems that some 'Aniza tribes reached these areas in the early eighteenth century. Other 'Aniza tribes then dispersed to other parts of Syria, becoming a majority of Syria's Bedouin.

In brief, researchers contend that Bedouin migrants who came to Palestine in the seventh century comprised the first of the three Bedouin migratory waves from the Arabian Peninsula into our region. Each migratory wave displaced previously resident tribes, which then dispersed into Syria, Iraq, and Palestine, or moved south to Egypt and North Africa. We know from various sources that from the time of the conquest of Palestine by the Islamic armies, until the second half of the nineteenth century, the tribes in the Sinai and Negev constantly fought both each other and invading tribes from the Arabian Peninsula (al-'Aref 1934: 9-34; Bailey 1980: 35-80, 1982: 131-64, 1985: 20-49; Sharon 1975: 11-30).

Within the Negev, the Bedouin were divided into clans, each of which consisted of several tribes sharing a common lineage. However, clans at times consisted of several tribes joined together for a common purpose, usually war.

During the four centuries of Ottoman rule (1516-1917), Palestine did not form an independent administrative unit. Palestine was divided into several districts, sanjaks, which were part of the Damascus (later Sidon) province, eyalet, which finally become part of the vilayet of Beirut. In the middle of nineteenth century, the sanjak of Jerusalem was elevated in status and organized as a mutasarriflik, an enlarged administrative unit, which also included the sanjaks of Nablus and Gaza, and was governed by a mutasarrif, usually a pasha with the rank of mirmiran. During the Crimean War this area was further raised to the status of an independent province. Its governor, a *pasha* with the rank of *vali*, was directly responsible to Istanbul.\It should be noted that Bedouin sheikhs, such as those of the Turabay family, ruled Jenin, Lajjun, and the Carmel area during part of the seventeenth century; and Dahir al-'Umar, of the Bedouin Zaydan family, was ruler of the Galilee for much of the eighteenth century (Ma'oz 1975: xv-xvi).\

During the Ottoman period, many Bedouin sheikhs and other local notables were nominated to be sanjak beys or sheikhs, and some of them were awarded feudal fiefs in return for their services. Some sheikhs were nominated for the position of guardian of certain important roads in the country (Sharon 1975). The Bedouin exacted protection payments from the sedentary population of the villages. This was a de facto system of taxation, referred to by villagers as injustice, (*mazlima*), and the Bedouin as *khawa*, 'brotherhood/brother right'. Until the nineteenth century, villages in Hawran were impoverished as a result of paying *khawa* to the Bedouin (Burckhardt 1831: 16-17, 299-307).

Such taxation, which remained in effect in some areas up to the twentieth century, and was prevalent throughout the nineteenth, was a material cause of the impoverishment of other areas as well. In the Middle East, the most common expression of the inferior status of one tribe compared to another is the payment of a tribute, also called *khawa*, to the stronger tribe. Sometimes, the Bedouin imposed it on travelers crossing their territory, a practice called *dira*. The tax was sometimes paid in the form of clothing and supplies. It was collected from most of the villages along the peripheries of the desert in Ottoman and early Mandatory times, but the mandatory authorities put an end to it (Jabbur 1995: 355-56, 611, al-'Aref 1934: 77-196).

Up to the early twentieth century, most semi-nomadic tribes on the outskirts of the Syrian Desert paid *khawa* to powerful tribes. The superior tribe that received the *khawa* undertook in exchange not to attack or raid the inferior tribe, to protect it from other tribes in case of attack or raid, to allow it to sojourn permanently within the boundaries of the superior tribe's territory, and to use its water and pasture land (Patai 1971: 253-63). Usually an inferior tribe paid *khawa* to a single superior tribe and therewith became its protected client. The Ruwala were the strongest of the 'Aniza tribes, their leaders considered the highest ranking dignitaries of the tribal leadership. They are called the heroes of *al-Jazira, shuj'an al-Jazira*.The Ruwala collected *khawa* from all the Hteym tribes, as well as from several villages lying on the outskirts of their tribal territory. Each tributary tribe and village had among the Ruwala its *akh*, 'brother', to whom it directly paid a certain annual sum. For this payment the *akh* gave protection and was bound to restore all property that fellow tribesmen may have taken (Musil 1928a: 59-60).

Usually the stigma of inferiority remained attached to a tribe long after it ceased to pay the *khawa* (Musil 1928a: 136). Tribes who used to pay *khawa* several generations ago, although they eventually acquired martial skills on a par with any Bedouin tribe, could not change their inferior social status. In the nineteenth century and early years of the twentieth, the Ottoman government paid a generous subsidy to the tribes along the pilgrim route, for safe conduct for the pilgrims (Kay 1978: 53-54). 'Abd al-'Aziz I forbade the Bedouin from taking the *khawa* from the pilgrimage caravans (Jabbur 1995: 516).

By the end of the nineteenth century, the Ottoman government had been able to attain a considerable degree of internal security in Palestine. With the reconstitution of Ottoman rule after the Egyptian conquest had ended—involving application of the *Tanzimat* (modernization) reforms, the institution of conscription, the establishment of a regular police force, and the construction of an efficient road and communications system—the Bedouin tribes had the choice of either withdrawing to the desert fastness or accepting the authority of the regime. Former belligerents began to work together in the new institutions—administrative, judicial, representative—established by the Ottomans, carrying on their former struggles by different means.

Nevertheless, Bedouin in the peripheral zones and desert areas would continue to demonstrate their independence from the authorities for decades to come. Many failed to pay taxes and internecine violence continued. All this was in addition to problems related to the border between Egypt and Palestine, which had been especially

acute in the early nineteenth century, when Muhammad 'Ali made
Egypt a semi-independent province. The border problem was exac-
erbated by the conquest of Egypt by Britain in 1882. The Ottomans
were unwilling to recognise not only British rule in Egypt, but also
Britain's inclusion of the Sinai Peninsula as part of Egypt. Matters
related to the Negev Bedouin were intimately linked to the question
of Ottoman control of the area. The Ottomans had a strong interest in securing the absolute loyalty of the sheikhs and the settlement
of the nomadic Bedouin tribes on the land. Such settlement would
have concurrently led to a reduction in bloodshed, an expansion
of areas under cultivation, and increased revenues for the public
exchequer. It was these considerations that led to the establishment
of the new district (qada) of Beersheba (Kushner 1995: 101-103;
Gerber 1985: 237-39).

Until the 1860s, the Ottoman authorities had more or less left
the Bedouin alone, save for occasional raids on tribes by government forces. In the 1860s, with the construction of the Suez Canal
(which was opened to passage in 1869), the Ottoman authorities
began to concern themselves with Egypt and to take measures to
impose order in the Negev. Inter-tribal wars were ruthlessly sup-
pressed and responsibility for the good behaviour of tribes was
placed upon the sheikhs (Marx 1967: 9-10). In the nineteenth century, the tribal life of the Negev's Bedouin was turbulent, as they
lived in a state of virtual independence from the nearest Ottoman
authorities, resident in Gaza (Bailey 1980: 35). But the Ottomans
embarked upon a systematic policy of pacifying the Bedouin, sending a penalty force to put an end to the disorders amongst them.

Pacification was implemented in three stages during the nineteenth century. In the forties and fifties, the Ottomans erected a
series of forts along the desert boundary. In the sixties and seventies,
they further strengthened the borders of the country by settling
Muslim groups with warlike traditions. The final stage consisted of
an attempt to settle the tribes by means of tax inducements and the
development of roads and telegraphic services. However, this policy
was not always successful (Avitsur 1976: 91-98; Gal-Pe'er 1979:
269-98). Palmer (1871: 389) describes how the governor of Syria,
Rashid Pasha, tried, circa 1870, to settle the Bedouin in the vicinity
of Gaza, ordering them to live in huts rather than tents. The Bedouin
resisted this threat to their nomadic way of life and killed fifteen of
the Ottoman troops sent to impose order. The Ottomans, in turn,

sent a penalty force, which confiscated Bedouin flocks. Eventually, the plan to settle the Bedouin in permanent buildings was thwarted by the viceroy of Egypt. In the mid-1880s, the *mutasarrif* of Jerusalem, Ra'uf Pasha, evinced concern over disorders in the south, which had even begun to threaten the Hebron area. He arrested sheikhs, confiscated flocks, and sent troops to the south, which only had the effect of exacerbating Bedouin animosity towards the government. Disorders and the subsequent dispatch of penalty forces constituted a vicious cycle.

The year 1891 has come to be known amongst the Bedouin as Year of Lemons (*sanat al-limoneh*). It was a drought year, and the Bedouin wandered north with their flocks, robbing the caravans of lemon merchants to feed themselves. The Ottomans sent a penalty force under Rif'at Bey to teach the Bedouin a lesson (al-'Aref, 1944:188-92). The *qaimaqam* (governor) of Gaza, 'father of tribes' Rustum Pasha, tried a different tack: he endeavoured to restore order by means of military raids. In 1894 he established a police and government station in the heart of tribal country, to which he also sent a garrison of troops and police, in order to bring the rule of law to the Negev. The permanent stronghold al-Juheir at Qal'et Futeis a wide cave located about nineteen km north-west of Beersheba, between the Tiyaha and Tarabin tribal areas overlooking the old road between Beersheba and Gaza, represents a new approach by the authorities towards the Bedouin, an approach which eventually led to the establishment of a central administrative centre in Beersheba. Thus was Beersheba founded in 1900, as the capital of the fifth subdivision (*Qada*) of the Jerusalem *mutasarriflik*, under a dignitary with the rank of Qaimaqam, as were the Qadas of Jaffa, Hebron, Jerusalem, and Gaza (al-'Aref 1934: 192, 244; Gal-Pe'er 1979: 269-98; Marx 1967: 31-32).

In embarking upon the above policy, the Ottomans had more in mind than just the welfare of the Bedouin and the prevention of inter-tribal bloodshed. Their reasons included a desire to expand their tax base and enlarge the population from which to raise troops. Second, Turkey was fearful that British and French domination over the Suez Canal would give them a foothold in the Near East; the Ottomans, for their part, were also interested in controlling the canal. The Muslim Bedouin could be allies of the Ottomans, as well as serve as a buffer between them and their enemies. Considerable diplomatic activity focused upon the Sinai Peninsula and the boundary between Egypt and the Ottoman Sultanate. The final boundary was fixed only in October 1906 (Shuqayr 1916: 588-616).

In order to improve their bargaining position, the Ottomans had to 'establish facts on the ground' in the Sinai Peninsula, which required the loyalty of the Bedouin. This had to be achieved by establishing an administrative unit, which would make the Ottoman presence felt, and by settling the Bedouin and distancing the tribal centre of gravity from Gaza (al-'Aref 1934: 244). Co-operation between the government and Bedouin had been manifest in the establishment of the town of Beersheba. According to a Bedouin tradition, the paramount chief (*'Aqid*) of al-'Azazma clan, Sheikh Hasan al-Malt'a, set out to persuade the Ottomans by moral suasion and gifts, to establish a police station to impose order and put an end to the long-festering warfare between his clan and the Tarabins.

The 'Azazma and Tarabin clans had clashed frequently over the years. After a series of battles in 1887 near what is now Beersheba, the 'Azazma had been driven into wastelands further south. Sheikh Hasan al-Malt'a, whose Mhemdiyin tribe owned the wells of Beersheba, asked the local Ottoman authorities for protection for his clan, he eventually went all the way up to the authorities in Istanbul. Towards this end, the sheikh donated his own large tent in 1896, which he pitched at what is now the *Saraya*, 'government house'. The first qaimaqam, Isma'il Kamal Bey (of Ottoman origin), held his office in that tent, which was placed on a hill overlooking Beersheba, until the Saraya was built. The architects responsible for planning the new city (Beersheba) were two Arab Palestinian engineers and two foreign engineers, one Swiss and one German. The Arab engineers were Sa'id Effendi al-Nashashiby and his assistant, Ragheb Effendi al-Nashashiby. The German served as a surveying officer in the Ottoman army (al-'Aref 1934: 245; Berman 1965: 315-16).

In the early years, rooms had been set aside in Saraya House, the Qaimaqamia, to serve as a municipal centre until a proper municipality was built. Over time, the internal division of that building was determined. On the top floor, a room was set aside for each of the following purposes: the District Court, the Tribal Court (*Mahkamat al-'Ashair*), and the office of the Qaimaqam. On the bottom floor, rooms were set aside for the office of the Magistrate's Court, the Muslim religious court, the superintendent of police, and the city clerk. In conclusion, one may say that in the first stage of construction (1900-1903), the Saraya House and several structures around it were built, as well as an army barracks and a centre for the gendarmerie. The second stage of the city's construction commenced in 1904, during the period of Qaimaqam Assaf Belge Bey the Damascene (1904-1906), and included construction of the municipality building, a mosque, and afterwards a two-storey school for Bedouin children, the first school in the Qada. Assaf Bey was distinguished by his hard work and the wide range of his activities. He was also known for the social events and ceremonies he held, to which he would invite the Bedouin from the surrounding region.

It is possible that the Bedouin request was only the pretext the Ottoman had been waiting for to establish the new administrative unit and Beersheba as its capital. The Bedouin have always considered the city's founding a positive development; they accepted the decision of the government at the time without any outward resistance. A Bedouin tradition tells of a conference of sheikhs which the authorities had convoked, at which the Ottomans received advice from the sheikhs, to which they accorded due consideration, and received the sheikhs' blessing for establishing Beersheba. In general, Bedouin traditions leave the strong impression that there was close co-operation between the Ottoman authorities and the tribal chiefs in founding the new city (al-'Aref 1934: 242-53; Bailey 1980: 35-80, 1982: 131-64; Marx 1967: 31-32).

The Ottomans established the administrative centre on the site of the ruins of Byzantine Beersheba for a number of reasons. To begin with, the site is central and the surrounding area, which is flatter than most of the Negev, has more fertile soil, and receives more precipitation as well; hence, the Beersheba Plain already contained a large Bedouin population (Marx, 1967:5-13). The area was under the control of a friendly sheikh al-Malt'a, which facilitated the government's functions of peace-keeping and monitoring Bedouin activities. The Tiyaha clan was located a few kilometres to the north, and the Tarabin a few to the west. The presence of ancient wells and the proximity to the surface of ground water, facilitating the digging of new wells, guaranteed that the administrative centre would not want for water, and in fact would be able to control an ancient inter-tribal irrigation area. The location also guaranteed the ability of the administration to control land transport, which passed along two ancient paths that crossed at Beersheba: the 'Aqaba-Gaza and the Hebron-'Aqaba roads. Other reasons for the choice of the site included Beersheba's sanctity to

Muslims, because of its connection to Abraham and Ishmael, as well as to 'Amro b. al-'Ass and his son 'Abdullah (famous Muslim fighters). Furthermore, caravans passed through the area, and in 1898 a khan had been built to accommodate wayfarers (al-'Aref 1934: 242-53; Bresslavsky 1946: 236-73; Gal-Pe'er 1979: 269-98). After Qaimaqam Isma'il Kamal Bey pitched the governor's tent in Beersheba and took control of the wells, the first measures taken were the cleaning out and fixing of the old wells, and the digging of two new ones. The old wells—Bir al-'Ukluk (Bir Ibrahim al-Khalil), Bir al-Shawwa, Bir al-Mufty, Bir al-Malt'a, and Bir al-Nashel—had previously been in use. The two new wells were al-Bir al-Saghir and Bir al-Jame'.

The public thoroughfares became safer and the region's commerce livelier, inter-tribal conflicts began to subside, and the surrounding area became more secure, for both the local Bedouin and caravans. One battalion of police and one of gendarmes, under an Albanian officer named Zobir Effendi, was put at the disposal of the Qaimaqam. So as to emphasise the authority of the Qaimaqam over the Bedouin, the famous sergeant, or shawish from Qal'et Futeis, Mustafa Effendi al-Arna'ut (Abu-Darwish, the Albanian), who had already proved his ability to rule the Bedouin, was appointed chief of gendarmes. He remained at his position until the end of the Ottoman period.

The second governor, Muhmmad Effendi Jaralla, expanded the governmental framework and put it on a sound footing. During his tenure, from 1900, work commenced on building the city and some of its public structures. The government purchased 2,000 *dunam*s (approximately 480 acres; there are 4.2 dunams to an acre) from the Mhemdiyin tribe of 'Azazma clan at the price of one *majidi* per dunam (one *Riyal majidi* was a Turkish silver coin of 20 piastres coined under Sultan Abdul Medjid), and registered them in its name at the Land Registry Office (*Kushan*). The construction of the government house (*Saraya*) was such that its windows overlooked the city's central street, and also afforded a view of the wells and of Wadi Beersheba. The main street had been built along the route of the road to Gaza southwards, and branched towards Hebron near Bir Ibrahim. A traveler from Gaza had to pass under the windows of the Saraya, and thus notice the highly obtrusive presence of the authorities.

Another public structure built during the tenure of the second governor was the barracks for policemen and gendarmes behind the

Saraya. The expenses related to the Saraya and the barracks were covered by means of government levies on the Bedouin. The government encouraged Bedouin to settle in the new city with land grants of one dunam; other settlers had to pay. Among the Bedouin on whose names lots were thus registered were: Hammad al-Sufy, Hasan al-Malt'a, 'Ali al-'Atawna and his son Hasan, Hasan Abu-'Abdun, Abu-Ghalyun, Hsein Abu-Kaff, Suweilem Abu-'Irfan, and the al-Rkaydy family. The sheikhs settled in the city, building large homes and stores for themselves. They would frequently go out to stay with their tribe-folk and return later to the city (al-'Aref 1934: 242-53).

In order to encourage the Bedouin to participate in government, the district governor established two councils: one to govern the district (al-Majles al-Idary) and the other to govern the city (al-Majles al-Balady). Both councils had Bedouin members. The district council included, in addition to government officials, sheikhs representing the five largest Negev clans, as follows:

Tarabin: Sheikh Waked al-Wuhaydy;
Hanajira: Sheikh Hamdan Abu-Hajjaj;
'Azazma: Sheikh Msallam Abu-Shannan;
Jubarat: Sheikh Harb al-Deqs;
Tiyaha: Sheikh Mhammad al-Sane', Qudeirat.

The municipal council also included five sheikhs who represented the same five Negev clans, as follows:

Tarabin: Sheikh Hammad al-Sufy, head of the council;
Hanajira: Sallam Abu-Zakry;
'Azazma: 'Awda Abu-Qbayleh;
Jubarat: Sliman Ibn Rafi';
Tiyaha: Hajj Hsein Abu-'Abdun (al-'Aref 1934: 242-53).

The authorities appointed one of the most important sheikhs, Sheikh Hajj 'Ali Sliman al-'Atawna, to the mayorship. He would to serve until his death in 1922. Beersheba began to serve as the centre of tax collection from the Bedouin, a function which the Ottoman authorities set out to streamline. They imposed taxes on agricultural produce, flocks of sheep, camels, salt, and on Bedouin tobacco. The taxes were collected through the sheikhs and tax agents. Beersheba also began to serve as a Muslim religious centre with the appointment of an Ottoman Qadi, one Shukry Effendi, whose job was that of a Muslim religious judge; it was the first such appointment in the region. The Qaimaqam Assaf Bey enhanced the religious status of the district capital in 1906 with the inauguration of a large and elaborate mosque, which came to symbolise co-operation between the Bedouin and Ottoman authorities. Negev Bedouin tribes had contributed over 1,000 pounds towards the mosque's construction. At the inauguration ceremony, the authorities held a great banquet for the Bedouin, at which their newborn sons were circumcised.

Among the other municipal functions by which Assaf Bey enhanced the attraction of the city for the Bedouin were an improved water system, construction of a flour mill, and the establishment of a post office and telegraph, housed in the Saraya. Most of the commercial activity was with the Bedouin who lived outside the city. Assaf Bey enhanced the commercial standing of the city with his establishment of an open livestock market and the setting of Wednesday as regional weekly market day. The establishment of the market engendered activity and commercial contacts, expanding the horizons of the Bedouin, who sold livestock, camels, sheep, and horses. Amongst the Bedouin there was particularly sharp demand for thoroughbred horses, which conferred considerable social standing. In addition, Assaf Bey built one of the most pleasant public buildings of the period, the district's first school, a two-storey structure. Several of the school's Bedouin graduates would eventually go on for further schooling in Istanbul (al-'Aref 1934: 33, 248; Bar-Zvi 1977: 28-31).

In 1908, administrative changes were made in the Negev, the aims of which were Bedouin participation in government. The Ottomans decided to improve the efficiency of their rule, and also to cultivate the loyalty of Bedouin in the Sinai, who had been separated for the previous year and a half from their brethren in Beersheba by an international border. The Ottomans never officially recognised the legality of the border the British had imposed. They fixed administrative points, the purpose of which was to enhance their rule over areas adjacent to the Sinai and its Bedouin population. Hence, they established an additional Qada adjacent to the Sinai, and began to build its administrative centre at 'Auja al-Hafir. The Qada at 'Auja was to be under the governor of Beersheba, 'Abd al-Karim Bey, and the deputy mutasarrif of Jerusalem, Rashid Bey Pasha. The overall plan was to raise the administrative status of

Beersheba from that of a district capital (Qada) to the capital of a sanjak divided into two districts, Beersheba and 'Auja, with both Qaimaqams under the deputy mutasarrif, resident in Beersheba. Aside from the administrative changes, the mutasarrif of Jerusalem, 'Ali Ekrem Bey (1906-1908), son of Namik Kemel, set out to bring the Bedouin closer to the government and capital city by means of generous presents and honours. Upon taking up his duties, he was instructed to pay particular attention to the Bedouin, and let them know of the Sultan's goodwill towards them.

While the Ottoman authorities in Palestine had long been pre-occupied with containing Bedouin raids into farming areas, and with the general unruliness common to the Bedouin, one could fairly say that by the second half of the nineteenth century, law and order had considerably improved in the country. Nevertheless, periodic clashes persisted, mainly in the desert areas. One such case that came to Ekrem Bey's attention was a bloody clash over cultivation rights between the Bedouin of Dhullam (Zullam), in the Negev, and the Hebron mountain village of Yatta. He resolved the dispute by transferring land to the Civil List (*chiflik*), and was able to report to his superiors at the Porte that both belligerent parties had found that solution satisfactory.

Yet more important than his resolution of individual disputes were Ekrem Bey's far-reaching administrative reforms in the desert region. Implemented in the area bordering on the British-controlled Sinai at the far south of the province, which was populated mainly by nomadic Bedouin tribes, these reforms were intended above all to reinforce the Ottoman presence. He effected this purpose by having the government institute a number of changes in the administrative divisions of the region. In Beersheba, for example, which had already been made a Qada, a Qaimaqam was appointed as 'assistant to the governor', elevating him above the other Qaimaqams. In addition, a new Qada was established in 'Auja al-Hafir and a new sub-district *nahiya* in Mulayha.

Beyond the administrative improvements, Ekrem Bey went on to present to the government a far-reaching proposal to settle the nomad Bedouin and register their lands, as a means of enhancing stability in the Negev. Furthermore, such a measure, by making possible increased production and more efficient tax collection, had the potential to significantly increase Treasury revenues. Here too, Ekrem Bey was able to inform his superiors at the Porte of success, as the Bedouin agreed to go along with the project, including the land registration. In retrospect, Ekrem Bey deserves credit for maintaining a fair degree of law and order in his jurisdiction. He instituted administrative reforms that served to enhance government control and make tax collection more efficient, considerable accomplishments (Kushner 1996: 349-62; al-'Aref 1934: 194-96, 242-53). The building of the administrative centre at 'Auja al-Hafir did not proceed as expected, though, while Beersheba reverted within a few months to its previous status of a Qaimaqamia. Al-'Aref (1934: 242-53) ascribes this change to the 'Young Turks' revolt of 24 July 1908, and to the subsequent shocks experienced by the Ottoman Empire.

Ekrem Bey, who was responsible for the comprehensive administrative reforms implemented in the Negev from the spring of 1908, saw a particularly urgent need to register the lands of the Bedouin, as part of their settlement process. Those reforms included the establishment of the new Qada of 'Auja al-Hafir and sub-district of Mulayha, and the promotion of the governor of Beersheba to assistant to the mutasarrif. In a visit to the Negev, Ekrem Bey informed the Bedouin himself of the pending reorganisation. During that visit, he presided over a mass circumcision of Bedouin babies; gave robes of honour, Qurans, and watches to the Bedouin sheikhs; and spoke of his plans for development of the region: importing cars, installing water pumps, and extending help with housing and obtaining loans. He told the assembled sheikhs and notables that cars would help the Bedouin market their agricultural products (al-'Aref 1934: 242-53; Hashkafa 1908).

The close relations between the Bedouin and the Ottoman authorities became evident in October 1914. In response to an Ottoman appeal, some 1,400 Negev Bedouin volunteered to join the forces (*Jardeh*) of Mumtaz Bey against the British at the Suez Canal. Bedouin participation in the Ottoman army was not widespread. Bedouin combatants mainly came from tribes whose sheikhs had shown particular loyalty to the Ottomans, especially those connected to Beersheba. Amongst those who led the Bedouin force were: Sheikh Hammad al-Sufy, who received the dignity of 'Basha' (Pasha) for his services to the Ottoman war effort, Sheikh Selim al-Zurei'y, Sheikh Sliman Abu-Setta, Sheikh 'Ali Abu-'Uwayly, Sheikh 'Arar al-Wuhaydy-Tarabin, Sheikh Hammad al-Sane', Sheikh Mansur Abu-S'eilik, Sheikh Hammad Abu-Shbab, Sheikh Jmay'an Ibn-Jermy, Sheikh 'Abd-Rabba Abu-'Ayadeh, Sheikh

Hasan al-Huzaiyil, Sheikh Salameh Abu-Shunnar, Haj Hasan Abu-'Abdun, Sheikh Ibrahim Abu-Irqaiyiq, Sheikh 'Abd-Alkarim al-Sane', Sheikh Salem 'Iyd Abu-Rabi'a, Sheikh Diab al-'Atawna, Sheikh Msallam Ibn-Sa'id al-'Azazma, Sheikh Sliman Ibn-Jkhaydem, Sheikh Frayj Ibn-Hamd, Sheikh Msallam Ibn-Khadira, Sheikh Mas'ud al-Wuhaydy al-Jubarat, Sheikh Harb al-Deqs, and Sheikh Nemr Abu al-'Udus. The Bedouin and Ottomans won the first battle which took place at Qatia; but in the second battle, at Ter'at al-Qantara, they suffered a severe defeat, and were forced to retreat (al-'Aref 1934: 248-53; Shuqayr 1916: 739-50).

The Ottoman government fixed the final tribal boundaries in the last year of its rule, 1917, and these remained in effect unchanged until 1949. A map was prepared indicating the area allotted to each tribe. Such fixing of clear boundaries perpetuated Beersheba as a central meeting point of the three main clans. The Ottomans also decreed that the ascension of each new sheikh required their authorisation; since they did not recognise dissident sheikhs, they effectively obviated tribal splintering (Marx 1967: 9-16).

It should be noted that after the founding of Beersheba and its becoming a military centre, external politics and war became the determining forces of Bedouin life. The employment of Bedouin in road and railway construction for the Ottoman army, and the great demand of both belligerents for camels and other beasts of burden, and for mutton, all contributed to material prosperity amongst the Bedouin during the First World War. This, in turn, had an impact on their lifestyle: they acquired assets, became less nomadic and more attracted to Beersheba and other military centres in the Negev. General Allenby began his Negev offensive in October 1917, and on the thirty first of the month took Beersheba (al-'Aref 1934: 245-48; Luke & Keith-Roach, 1930: 27).

It would seem that the establishment of Beersheba and its tribal school is one of the few examples on record where the Ottoman government intentionally established an urban settlement. Another rare example, albeit an essentially different one, is the establishment of the two towns of Nasiriyyah and Ramadi in Iraq, by Midhat Pasha (Gerber 1985: 238; Longrigg 1925: 306-9). They, too, were established in order to serve as centres for settled Bedouin populations (Jamali 1934: 56-57).

The Negev is some 12,000 sq.km in area, 60 per cent of the total area of Israel. The Bedouin live in the Beersheba valley, over an area of about 1,000 sq.km, 400 of which consist of cultivated lands; the remaining 600 sq.km are pasturelands. Before the establishment of the State of Israel, the Negev Bedouin cultivated agricultural lands extending over some 2,000 sq.km, growing barley, wheat, sorghum, watermelon, lentils, broad beans, citrus, vines, apples, apricots, almonds, figs, olives, and pomegranates (Abu-Rabi'a 1994a: 7-9).

Chapter 2

Ottoman Education

Public education in Palestine before World War I was essentially as it had originally been established under the Ottoman law of 1869. The secondary and higher elementary schools in the provinces were subject to *vilayet* control under Imperial officers, and were relatively efficient. The lower schools in the towns and villages, managed by special local committees, were often little better than the old *Kuttab* schools (lower elementary schools). The school system was based on the French model. Improvements in organization and efficiency were made after the revolution of 1908, especially after the enactment of a 1913 law designed to strengthen the control of the Ministry and Imperial education officers over the lower elementary schools. The northern sub-districts of Palestine, which were part of the vilayet of Beirut, profited more than the autonomous Sanjak of Jerusalem, where education was largely in the hands of foreign missionary bodies and the law of 1913 was virtually a dead letter. In theory, Ottoman public education was free and compulsory, although universal elementary education for Muslims never became a reality in any part of the Empire. Religious instruction was part of the curriculum, and some provision was made in the law for religions other than Islam. In general, it would be fair to say that the public schools in the Ottoman provinces were poorly organised and the methods of instruction unsatisfactory.

Up to the outbreak of the First World War, Turkish was the medium of instruction in public schools. The use of Turkish, a foreign language in Palestine, combined with the basic defects mentioned above to render the schools largely ineffective (al-Haj 1995:

37-41; Erskine 1935: 198-221; Luke & Keith-Roach 1930: 236-38; Mar'i 1978; Szyliowicz 1973: 151-169; Tibawi 1956: 19-41). In 1911 the school-age population was estimated at 38,053 boys and 35,584 girls. Government schools had attendance of 6,104 boys and 1,504 girls, while private and foreign schools had 6,974 boys and 2,673 girls. This meant that 25,000 boys and 13,400 girls had no chance of learning to read, that only 34 per cent of boys and 12 per cent of girls attended schools (Abcarius, 1946:101).

In Palestine in 1914 there were 98 state schools (95 elementary and 3 secondary) with a total of 234 teachers and 8,248 pupils (only 1,480 girls) in all. It was partly as a concession to Arab national feeling that a higher secondary school where Arabic was used as a medium of instruction in addition to Turkish, established in Jerusalem during the First World War. This school also served as a training college.

According to the Ottoman estimate in 1914, the number of private Muslim schools was 379, with 417 teachers and 8,705 pupils (only 131 girls). The great majority of these Muslim schools were of the traditional *kuttab* type. *Kuttab*s were conducted in private houses or mosques, and children roughly between the ages of five and twelve were taught by sheer repetition to learn by heart the whole Quran, the precepts of Islam, reading, writing, and arithmetic. Those who taught in them were men educated in mosque circles or at best in al-Azhar University in Cairo. They naturally taught through the medium of Arabic, and charged modest fees but received no state assistance, and were not under any strict state inspection (Tibawi 1956: 8, 20, 56-57). When the state finally took the initiative and came to exercise some control, it directed all attention to higher education and left all elementary education in the hands of private individuals or groups, who developed this peculiar type of private school.

The Tribal School in Istanbul

Sultan Adb al-Hamid II ascended to the Ottoman throne (1876-1909) during a very difficult period. War with Russia was about to break out, and the Ottoman Empire's outlying provinces were in turmoil. The outcome of the war with Russia induced certain developments that help explain a growing interest in the Arab provinces, and a desire to create a viable basis of social solidarity between

Ottoman and Arab, to enable the survival of the Empire (Akarli 1986: 74-89; Rogan 1996: 83-107).

Since the late 1830s, ministers with Western ideas had been increasingly influential at the Porte, which had commenced a long-term reorganisation (*Tanzimat*, or modernisation). The resulting interest in the Arab provinces led the government of the Porte to adopt a policy that hinged on local notables, through whom the Porte dealt with the population at large. The application of such a policy perforce varied by region, between city and hinterland, and with the level of sedentarisation of the local population. Urban notables, whose sons were educated in Istanbul, obtained government offices and became loyal members of the governing elite (Akarli 1986: 74-89; Hourani 1968: 41-68; Khoury 1983: 50-55; Sadat 1969: 13-32).

In October 1892 Sultan Adbulhamid II established the *Asiret Mekteb-i Humayun*, or Imperial School for Tribes. It was a five-year secondary boarding school that 'selected from among the physically and mentally gifted boys, between twelve to sixteen-year-old, those who belonged to respectful families of the various Arab tribes'. A quota was specified for each Arab province. The students were to be on full government scholarship, including a monthly stipend. Graduates were expected to rejoin their tribes and to serve as teachers or officials in their area.

Most of those who entered the military rose to the rank of captain, and some higher. Of the smaller number who entered the civil service, most attained district governorships. Some of the civil servants eventually attained the rank of pasha, and some were elected to Parliament.

Asiret Mektebi was closed in February 1907, after a student riot. It should be noted that in the Jerusalem district, there were six Bedouin students. Two of them withdrew or were expelled. The other four students were Jabar Jawdat Humud Wahidat, Sulayman 'Ayd Abu 'Ayd Hanajira, Ahmad Salim Abu Kishk, and Mahmud Tughan (Dhughan) Sawalima (Rogan 1996: 83-107).

Tribal School in Beersheba

After Beersheba was established with its governmental framework expanded and the city put on a standard municipal footing, work commenced on building some of its public structures. Beersheba had begun to serve as a Muslim religious centre. The Qaimaqam, Assaf Belge Bey the Damascene, enhanced the regional status of the district capital in 1906 with his inauguration of a large and elaborate mosque. He also built one of the most pleasant public buildings of the period, the district's first Bedouin tribal school, consisting of two storeys and sixteen rooms. During the construction of the school, Bedouin students studied in a small room or tent as a Kuttab. They were taught reading, writing Arabic, the Quran, and arithmetic. This privilege was for the sons of sheikhs, dignitaries and notables who lived in Beersheba or its periphery.

One should bear in mind that Beersheba's hinterland population consisted of several tens of thousands of Bedouin, whom the Ottomans wanted to instruct, especially in agriculture, and thus render more disciplined citizens. The selectivity of admission to the school must also be noted; most of its pupils were the sons of sheikhs and dignitaries. Such men were wont to send their sons cities such as Gaza to get an education. At this stage, education was not the lot of the ordinary Bedouin, but only of the tribal elites. Hence, education accentuated existing tribal stratification by helping to perpetuate the leadership class. Several sheikhs' sons studied at the Beersheba school, and the brighter amongst the graduates were eventually sent on for further schooling in Istanbul (Hamd Abu-Taha, Personal communication, 9 February 1984; al-'Aref 1934: 248; Bar-Zvi 1977: 28-31). Their parents were very anxious, due to their belief that the Ottomans wanted to induct their sons into the army. They made every effort, including bribes (*bakhshish*) to officials, to bring their sons back before they completed their study at Istanbul; most succeeded (Bar-Zvi, 1977: 29). Other sheikhs and notables refused to send their sons to Istanbul, for the above reason (Hamd Abu-Taha, Personal communication, 9 February 1984). According to oral interviews with Bedouin, among the students who were sent to the school at Istanbul were:

1. Hamd Hamdan al-Sane', from Najamat al-Sane' of Tarabin;
2. Ibrahim Mhammad al-Sane', from Qudeirat al-Sane' of Tiyaha;
3. Mhammad 'Ibyd Abu Suhayban , from Najamat of Tarabin;
4. Sliman Ghayth Abu-Ghalyun, from Jarawin of Tarabin;

For more details about the above-mentioned four students, see Chapter 6.

At the Beersheba school too, the Bedouin were instructed in reading, writing, religion, and some agriculture, with the aim of facilitating their settlement in the land. The government endeavoured, with no success, to establish an agricultural school in 1906, although plans for such a school had been maintained by the Ottomans until the end of their rule (al-'Aref 1934: 247; Bresslavsky 1946: 50). The school had originally been planned as an agricultural school for Bedouin children, where they were to have undergone change from nomads to workers of the land. This had been the intention of the Ottoman governors already in the first years of the city's existence. Ekrem Bey, the mutasarrif in Jerusalem in the years 1906-1908 (Alsberg 1975: 537; Kushner, 1996: 349-62), made these intentions known to an assembly of sheikhs during an official visit to Beersheba in 1908 (al-'Aref 1934: 247; Gal-Pe'er 1991: 89-92; see Appendix-1). In order to facilitate attendance for the more distant tribes, the school built a boarding school towards the end of 1913.

The school was built in a manner typical for public buildings at the time. It was spacious, consisted of two storeys, and had a shingle roof. It was symmetric and had a central entrance through a lobby which had three arches overhead, and which opened into a large central hall.

When the First World War broke out in 1914, Beersheba served as the Ottoman command centre, where supply and transportation facilities were located along with workshops, warehouses, and sundry other installations used by the army. There were large military forces in the area, and the school building was converted into a Red Crescent hospital, for which purpose it had undergone refurbishing, and soon began to receive patients. Most of the patients were not wounded, but victims of plagues that ravaged the Ottoman army. In the winter of 1916, epidemics of cholera and typhus devastated the Ottoman ranks. In order to ease the load, a field hospital was established in tents behind the mosque; it served mainly German and Austrian personnel (Gal-Pe'er 1991: 89-92). General Allenby began his offensive in October 1917, and on the 31st of the month had taken Beersheba (al-'Aref 1934: 245-48; Luke and Keith-Roach 1930: 27).

The new political and modern conditions have increased the rapidity of change in the material, socio-economic and intellectual life of the Bedouin. Education was the main factor for adaptation and adjustment to the new conditions. It should be noted that most of the graduates of the tribal school at Beersheba succeeded their fathers to become famous sheiks, governmental officials, businessmen, and the leaders of the Bedouin tribes in the Negev.

It should be noted that in 1914 the Ottoman authoriries estimated the total population (Arabs and Jews) of Palestine at 689,275 (Luke and Keith-Roach 1930: 39). On the establishment of the British civil administration in 1920, the total population was some 700,000 (one-tenth Jewish). In 1948 when the British mandate was terminated the official estimate of the Arab population was just over 1,300,000 and of the Jewish population just over 600,000.

Appendix 1

Speech of Ekrem Bey to Negev Bedouin Sheikhs

Arab [Bedouin] elders and inhabitants!

Gather and come to me and hear in your mind's ear, and lend your ears to my words. I am your governor, I am your father, and I am your brother, who will hold forth to you. There is a message for you on my lips today. Joy and gladness. I hereby come to your joy, because you are the contented servants, who find grace in the sight of the Lord, who has created the high and majestic mountains, the wilderness and the desert, the clouds, the skies, the sun and the stars, in one word, has created all the creatures from nothing. He is the God who blessed your excellent horses with the speed of the wind. It is He who has blessed your grain yield with their grain's abundance, you with health of body and your climate with a pleasantness as delightful as that of the Garden of Eden. So it is. The Lord has indeed been revealed to you in His prayers, His loving-kindnesses, and His favours. For what? Because you are perfect and on your brow shines the light of the Islamic religion and a bountiful sanctity. Your tongue is the tongue of the Quran and your religion that of enlightened knowledge. You are contented ones who often raise the word of the One God from your mouths. The saying 'There is no God but God and Muhammad is His prophet' is displayed on your brows, as a sun to the pure faith, thank God and the faith of Islam. You are contented because the merciful God blesses you in this climate, the skies of which shall produce the light of life. Your land is as broad as its skies. In whom resides grace and divine influence, a love for the land and its treasure. And it is true as day that even with easy work you are able to take from it yields that suffice not for you alone, sons of Beersheba, but also for Jerusalem, even for all of Syria, who number over a million souls. And all this is from your fruitful land and the pleasant air of your country. Yes. It is true that you also have some hot places, but for the most part, the air is temperate, and every day the sun shall send its warm rays on to your land and the clouds of the sky shall pour on it the pearls of dew that give life. And that is truly the way it is, because the light of your Beersheba sun is nothing but the sun of life. In your wildernesses will not be found a region marked by swamps and lakes of water, and temperate air prevails over all the spaces of the land. And in one word I can say that our lives are pleasant lives; from this place we can get an idea of the World to Come, of the Garden of Eden. The good Lord blesses you with great abundance, with varieties of grass that luxuriate in this beautiful climate. You are contented. For what? Because you are as your other believing brethren, whose number will rise to several millions sheltered in the shadow of benevolence and graciousness of His Majesty our lord, vicar of the Prophet Muhammad, who avails himself of the aid of the king of kings, blessed be He, who fears God, the king of believers and the most perfect, the victorious Sultan son of a Sultan, His Majesty Abd al-Hamid, may his honour be raised. So may one imagine a contentedness greater than this great contentedness? God forbid! Long live His Honour our exalted and glorious king. He is supported in his strength with victorious marshals of armies. They are as rows of angels, as the dwellers of heaven. His heart, filled with the spirit of holiness, is a light to Faith. It is hence incumbent upon all to know and to believe with complete faith that the rank of our great Sultan and King is supreme and exalted and above the thoughts of all created beings. Bedouin tribes and elders of Ottoman! All which I shall clarify and interpret for you cannot describe the image of honour and glory of our great King and the titles of our exalted Sultan. Is it possible for us to number the stars in the skies? Or is the light of the sun what is required as an example? Arab elders! By God it is clear that the Sultanic guidance and the great benevolence that distinguish His Majesty the Sultan, may his honour be raised, are as heaven, which has no limit or measure.

Hear me, O Arab [Bedouin] elders. Understand my words with the strength of your hearts and the honesty in your hearts, for I have come to explain to you the new arrangements in Beersheba, and at the same time I shall explain to you the kindnesses and favours you have been privileged to receive, beyond those of your other faithful brethren. His Majesty our lord the Sultan has issued his high edict to render the centre of Beersheba to be a *mutassarif* by Pasha Muauneit, and the higher official in your city is Abd el-Karim Bey, and, in accordance to the rank of the office of the highest official, the ranks of the other officials have also been raised. It has also been decided to establish in Beersheba a large school for the work of the land, because you are certainly diligent people. Lack of knowledge in the science of work of the land prevents you from making your fertile land productive. Some of you have no doubt journeyed to Jaffa and seen with your own eyes the conditions of how the land is worked there, and that is because there are people there learned in this profession, who come to the point where their land produces forty or fifty measures. You as well, if you only learned the ways to work, you would be able to acquire great benefit. In this school, your children will learn how to sow and how to reap. Your bosoms will fill with gold and silver, as much as the sheaves of barley. No doubt your sons will learn to read the holy Quran and the law of the enlightened religion, and how to worship our Maker. So too they will learn how to proceed and present tokens of your work at the footstool of our lord His Majesty the Sultan, may his honour be raised, who has been good to you. Pray at the mosque in Beersheba, and thus fulfill your obligations to religion, and you will thus come to recognise the benevolence of our lord His Majesty the Sultan, may his honour be raised. This school is a benevolence and charity from our lord, our King to you, and you will glory in it. This glory is not limited to Beersheba, but rather extends to Jerusalem and its environs, as well. And you shall see your sons and be joyous and respect them for the breadth of their knowledge and wisdom. I shall also build you in Beersheba a tower and a clock, so that you may know the time for prayer and the time for work. I shall build you a bathhouse to wash and purify your bodies for the benefit of your health. Beersheba no longer has a mill. Therefore, I shall establish mills for the milling of your wheat, and an oven will likewise be established where you can bake your dough. Just as this settlement will expand shortly, so shall large houses and palaces be built. Yet because of the distance from the centre of the places in which you sow your seeds and the places of residence of your tribes, clearly you suffer much in bringing your produce to Beersheba and coming from such a long distance. Hence, our lord His Majesty the Sultan, may his honour be raised, has already ordered the establishment of a new *Qada* and *Nahiya* in the vicinity of Beersheba, and in accordance with your advice, after we had examined all the places together with you, the place al-'Auja has been selected for the new *Qada* centre. In this place will be built a government building, a mosque, a field for the army, a telegraph station, and homes for the officials. And these institutions and buildings will be made by the government of His Majesty. Furthermore, a Sultanic decree has been sent out to support with cash any builder of a home in the new centre. And soon I shall announce to you the amount of this money in such a manner that any amongst you who wish to built a home in al-'Auja shall receive actual support. We shall also dig wells for you and bring their waters up in machines to Beersheba, so that the waters shall come up from the ground to irrigate this plain and this broad square, until it will be easy to plant trees and vineyards and orchards. In al-Mulayha a centre and Nahiya have been established, and there an official ready to answer the first call for help will be appointed.

Elders and Arabs! [Bedouin] You are all farmers for whom the work of the land is as the soul of life, and according to the measure of the development of your land, so will grow your success and happiness. And should you be helped for ten or fifteen years, to prepare you to know what you lack, then your seed will develop abundantly, without limit, and you shall possess wealth and riches noted throughout the world. We have troubled ourselves to advance improvements in matters aside from those in which you had felt you were in want. Even in those matters that had never even occured to you. Hearken and listen. Thus far, I have explained to you the great benefit contained in a school for the work of the land. And in addition to that, his Majesty, who has the seed and the power, our lord the Sultan son of a Sultan, may his honour be raised, has commanded this day to satisfy your every need so as to sustain you. He has ordered to open in Beersheba a branch of the special bank for farmers, and is willing to make emendations in the laws of that bank, in this place, so that it will be easy to obtain loans. And you will thus be saved from the hands of the money changers and leasers of your land, and you will be able to add to your livelihood, and the tools and implements of your work. So too the government of His Majesty, may his honour be raised, is willing to bring all the tools of the kind used in Jaffa, to plough, to plant seed, and to render your land fruitful, and land that now yields you twenty measures will yield you a hundred measures. You see today that your camels go back and forth and you suffer very much from that, and because of the difficulty of transporting your yield from place to place, you are forced to leave the fruit of your land where it grows, and thus you cannot plant much seed. Therefore, we are also providing for that want, and this year already we are prepared to bring an 'automobile machine' from time to time; and it will be explained to you what an automobile is and how it works and can bring your yield from place to place. That machine will make its way from al-'Auja to Beer-sheba, at one or two o'clock, and you will load your produce on it and it shall carry it as lighting, as clouds carry rain. Today will serve as an example for many in the bright future that awaits you.

His Majesty, our lord the Sultan, may his honour be raised, has issued the order to implement these new arrangements in Beersheba. He is our lord who has been kind enough to enlighten your minds with the light of this sun, and will make your hearts pleasant in the beauty of the delight of springtime. He is our lord the Sultan, may his honour be raised, who has ordered you be shown his kindnesses and clothed in fine clothes, and soon I shall give you these gifts and clothe you with my own hands.

Elders and Arabs [Bedouin]! Son of our lord and benefactor, our God-fearing Sultan, may his honour be raised, the high and glorious, maintainer of the enlightened religion and beloved vicar of God, king of believers. Our lord and Sultan has commanded me to give to each man, each man of you, one Quran, so that the new arrangements may be effective as the effectiveness of laws of the holy Quran. Kiss this holy book with feelings of holiness from the depth of your hearts, and pray with your pure and blessed devotion, with pure Bedouin hearts, for the well-being of our lord the Sultan, may his honour be raised, who has deigned to immerse you in a sea of right-eousness and munificence, and who will be revealed to your eyes in grace and mercy, and great compassion, and who has restored you to contentment, to live a life of happiness. Pray a prayer that is not short and say and repeat thrice, 'Long live His Majesty our King the Sul-tan, may his honour be raised' (Hashkafa no. 71, 1908).

Reply of the Sheikhs

Upon completion of the speech by His Excellency the Minister Pasha, may his honour be raised, it was translated into the Arabic language by Sheikh Ali Effendi el-Hamawi. The Arab [Bedouin] elders forthwith sent a telegram to His Majesty our lord the Sultan, may his honour be raised, the translation of which is as follows:

King of the believers and chief of the perfect ones, you are our King and Sultan, you are to us a symbol and image of grace, a merciful one who fills with mercy, you whose fountain of enlightened wisdom, a light unto the world, has burst forth on the life of our tribes as the light of dawn. You in whose enlightened government is found the book of God's Law. You who have restored us to life with your sultanic decree, derived from the primal decree of God from on high. You who have raised our worth with your sultanic loving-kindness and beneficence. You who have slaked us with the revealed dewdrops of your redeeming compassion and shall clothe us with the magnificence of your generosity, and convey us to those on high under your view and your exalted supervision. You also made a gift to us of the enlightened Law, the divine gift, the most perfect of the heavenly books, to which no price may be affixed. It is true that you have fulfilled the divine injunction, 'God shall command to do what is right and kind' to your Arab [Bedouin] servants, who shall fulfill with a full heart the divine injunction, 'Listen to the Lord, listen to the Prophet and to My lord amongst you'. These new arrangements are nothing but the fruit of your generosity and pleasantness, and the glory of your throne. Everything is from your loving-kindness. You are our high and exalted lord, king of perfection and vicar of the Divine Prophet, who have deigned to restore to human beings life. As for us, what is there for us but to bow at your honoured feet and come to the gates of your exalted government? You are our benefactor and king. And what songs would it be becoming for our mouths to utter? We are protected under your shadow. We are your Arab servants. You who have slaked our land with the dewdrops of the salvation of your kindness, who have spread your loving-kindness over our tents. You have sent a new light on to our hearts, you have covered us with your hidden compassion, and you shall send to al-Hafir and al-Mulayha the perfume of your supervision. You have gladdened your orphans and have made pleasant for our sakes and for our camels and beast of burden. We do not have the power of tongue to express our gratitude to you for your beneficence to us, or to give expression to the feelings of our hearts. Hence, you our lord, King of the believers and priest of the two holy houses, we have nothing to present at your feet but the pleasantness of our pure prayers, which come from a pure heart, and say, 'God keep our victorious Sultan and lord, son of a Sultan, Abd al-Hamid, may his honour be raised'.

On the twenty-eighth day of Nisan, in the year one thousand three hundred twenty-six. Your servants the Arab elders of Beersheba (Hashkafa, no. 72, 1908).

Appendix 2

Beersheba's Governors: Qaimaqams

The governors of Beersheba during Ottoman times were:
Isma'il Kamal Bey, Muhmmad Afendi Jaralla, Tawfik Bey al-Ghassin (deputy), Hamdy Bey, Tawfiq Afendi 'Abd al-Hady, Salem Afendi Tahbub (deputy), Assaf Belge Bey the Damascene (1904-1906), Farid Afendi al-'Umary, 'Abd al-Karim Bey, 'Ali Assaf Afendi the Turk, Mahmud Nadim Bey, 'Irfan Bey al-Jaby, Khalid Bey, Kamel Afendi al-Bdiry (deputy), Husam al-Din Bey, and Sadeq Bey al-Maghreby (al-'Aref 1934: 245-48).

Chapter 3

Bedouin under British Mandate

General Edmund Allenby began his operation in October1917, and on the thirty first of the month, at 6 p.m., Beersheba surrendered to him. Capt. B. B. Ragless was appointed the city's first military governor (al-'Aref 1934: 254-63; Luke and Keith-Roach 1930: 27). During the British Mandate (1917-1948) Beersheba remained capital of the Qada and administrative centre of the Bedouin population, serving as a unifying factor which engendered a feeling of political belonging. The British drew the boundaries of the Qada so that it included all the Negev Bedouin, making the city in effect the capital of all Bedouin in southern Palestine. Beersheba had also become the seat of the Qaimaqam, who would be chosen because he knew Arabic and admired the Bedouin lifestyle, which had captivated many of the British. Officers serving in the district guaranteed public order and Bedouin loyalty by forging personal ties with the tribes, including frequent visits to their encampments, and by mediating between the Bedouin and higher authorities. With Beersheba serving as a base, the British deployed their forces throughout the Bedouin region, keeping the peace more effectively than the Ottomans had. The British did not try to impose British laws on the Bedouin, but rather endeavoured to 'institutionalise' Bedouin law. Towards that end, Beersheba also became a juridical centre, in addition to an administrative centre for the authorities (Gal-Pe'er 1979: 269-98).

In the Negev, as elsewhere, the British employed the method of indirect rule, by which they availed themselves of the existing structure of the subject society and its laws, to which they had granted legitimacy, provided these did not contradict British law. The British used Bedouin tradition and laws, and the hierarchical structure within the tribes, as the means of imposing order. At the outset of the Mandate, the authorities chose seven sheikhs, representing the five principal Negev clans, to serve as council of advisors, *'Umad* (*'Umda*, sing.), with whom they consulted on economic affairs, and to whose advice they were wont to lend weight. The government assigned two policemen, at its expense, to each *'Umda*. The policemen were directly responsible to the *'Umad*. However, this arrangement lasted only some six months, because the *'Umad* used the policemen for their own purposes. Hence, the government revoked the assignment of the policemen. The seven *'Umad* were:

Tarabin: Hmeid Basha al-Sufy and Hsein Abu-Setta;
Tiyaha: Salman al-Huzaiyil and 'Ali al-'Atawna;
Hanajira: Freih Farhan Abu-Meddein;
Jubarat: Su'ud al-Wuheidy;
'Azazma: Salameh Ibn-Huwayshel.

At least two of the above, Hajj 'Ali al-'Atawna and Hmeid Basha al-Sufy, were long-time residents of Beersheba, the first-named having been mayor since the city's founding and the second, his successor. Third member was the Hanajira tribal leader Sheikh Freih Farhan Abu-Meddein, who had served the British in the First World War, built his home in Beersheba, and even served briefly as the city's mayor in the early 1920s.

Bedouin sheiks and leaders who came to Jerusalem to greet Sir Herbert Samuel, the High Commission, refused to countenance the efforts of Arab nationalists to persuade them to protest against the British rule in Palestine (Wasserstein 1991:90). Samuel established an Advisory Council consisting of eleven officials and ten non-officials, all nominated by him. The ten non-officials comprised four Muslims, three Christians and three Jews. It should be noted that Sheikh Freih Abu-Meddein was one of the four Muslims; he represented the Bedouin tribes in South Palestine. The first meeting of the Advisory Council took place on 6 October 1920 (Wasserstein 1991: 93; PRO FO 371/51/149).

After the occupation of Beersheba, the British Government established what are known as the Tribal Courts (*Mahkamat al-'Ashair*). At the outset, these courts were not regularly constituted, and it seemed that any sheikh in the tribe was entitled to sit in one.

Magisterial warrants were not issued to the individuals. This state of affairs lasted only two years. The Palestine Government then put the Tribal Courts on a more satisfactory basis. It limited the number of sheikhs qualified to serve as judges, and also limited the number of courts. Section 45 of the Palestine Order in Council published by order of the King in the Gazette of 1ˢᵗ September 1922, reads as follows: 'The High Commissioner is empowered to establish Tribal Courts in Beersheba or in any tribal area where he thinks fit. These Tribal Courts are entitled to apply tribal customs insofar of justice'. Members of the Tribal Courts were appointed, numbering sixteen, from the main clans, as follows:

> Tarabin: Hsein Abu-Setta, 'Abd-Rabba Abu al-Hssayn,
> Hamd al-Sane', Hajj Hmeid al-Sufy, Nemr al-Wuheidy;
> Tiyaha: Salman al-Huzaiyil, Hasan al-'Atawna, Hsein
> Abu-Kaff;
> Dhullam: Khalil Salem Abu-Rabi'a (Irbay'eh);
> 'Azazma: Sliman Ibn-Jkhaydem, Salameh Ibn-Huwayshel,
> Nasser Abu al-Khayl;
> Hanajira: Freih Abu-Meddein, Selim al-Smeiry;
> Jubarat: Hasan Abu-Jaber, Nemr Abu al-'Udus.

They were not even asked to take the oath of allegiance. But in 1923 these defects were remedied when High Commissioner Sir Herbert Samuel visited Beersheba for the swearing in of the Tribal Court judges. During this visit, he also set a fee for the tribal judges, at 200 mills a sitting. The authority of the Tribal Court, which had been intended to deal mainly with infringements of Bedouin law and custom, was expanded in 1928 to include adjudication of criminal offences which entailed penalties of not more than three months in gaol, or fines not in excess of 50 Palestine pounds.

The room in which the Tribal Courts sat was located on the upper storey of the Saraya building (Qaimaqamia), near the District Court, which helped to further impress Beersheba on Bedouin minds as the seat of justice and governmental laws. In practice there was a tendency for all the judges to sit in the one court room at the same time. This involved delays, though it was profitable for judges of the Court. In 1924, the number of members permitted to sit in court at once was limited to three. If there was a need for several Courts to sit this was permitted. The Tribal Courts were entitled to deal with cases where a litigant lived in Beersheba, or property concerned was in the sub-district. If both parties were townspeople, their cases were dealt with by the Civil Magistrate, not the Tribal Court. From 22 December 1932, Tribal Court decisions were subject to appeal to a tribunal consisting of the Qaimaqam as president, and two judges of the Tribal Courts who were not at the original hearing (al-'Aref 1933: 62-69; 1934: 271).

The Bedouin court system also employed an investigating officer—*Mustanteq*—whose duty it was to investigate conflicts between tribes and inform the Qaimaqam and police chief of the results of the investigation. A resident of Beersheba, the Bedouin Hajj Sliman Ghayth Abu-Ghalyun, held the position of Mustanteq under Sheikh Hsein Abu-Kaff (Bar-Zvi 1977: 1-13).

Another juridical body established by the British in Beersheba, which functioned from 1919 to 1922, was the 'Blood Council' (*Majles al-demum*), for the settlement of blood feuds between Bedouin. The Majles al-demum members were Sheikhs of the five principal Negev clans, as follows:

Tarabin: Sheikh Hsein Abu-Setta, and Sheikh Hmeid al-Sufy;
Tiyaha: Sheikh Ibrahim Abu-Irqaiyiq, and Sheikh Salameh
    Abu-Shunnar;
Hanajira: Sheikh Freih Abu-Meddein;
'Azazma: Salameh Ibn-Huwayshel;
Jubarat: Su'ud al-Wuheidy.

This council adjudicated over 150 blood feuds and ransom cases before it was abolished and its functions taken over by the Tribal Court in 1922. Council meetings were headed by the mayor, Sheikh 'Ali al-'Atawna (al-'Aref 1933: 62-69).

The prominence of Beersheba as a Bedouin juridical centre was particularly noticeable during the tenure of al-'Aref as Qaimaqam (1929-39). He had previously gained experience amongst the Bedouin tribes in the Transjordan, understood the Negev Bedouin, gained their confidence, and had become close to them. Al-'Aref enhanced the juridical efficiency of the Qada capital, and succeeded in making Bedouin law less severe and bringing it into line with the law of the state. This was accomplished by means of a gradual adoption of a system of fines in respect of various offences, instead of capital or corporal punishment, which Bedouin judges had hitherto imposed. As far as continuation of ordeal-by-fire (which consisted of licking a flame, the practice of *besh'a*) to determine a man's guilt or innocence, al-'Aref had the seat of the *mubashshe'* (the man who practicing the besh'a) transferred to Beersheba, where the urban milieu had the effect of inhibiting continued practice of the besh'a. And indeed, the practice of besh'a declined dramatically over the years. Another of al-'Aref's reforms was his prohibition of lawyers taking up residence in Beersheba, thus sparing innocent Bedouin from being fleeced in unnecessary ligation and lawsuits (al-'Aref 1944: 116-124; Avitsur 1976: 97; Ginat 2000).

In order to preserve law and order amongst the Bedouin, the British established a special mobile police force, the Palestine Gendarmerie, based in Beersheba. Gendarmerie personnel would patrol the expanses of the Negev by horse and camel, to make the force's presence felt. Police riding camels were known as *hajjaneh* (sing. *hajjan*). The famous genre of Bedouin poetry known as *hjiniy* is attributed to the songs of the hajjan riding his camel (Bailey 1991).

The purview of hajjaneh responsibilities included combatting criminal activity, preventing the carrying of firearms north of a specified line, combatting smuggling, and reporting disturbances to headquarters in Beersheba. The force was composed almost entirely of Bedouin, with the upper echelons coming from the families of sheikhs. Each unit policed its own tribal area; the policemen thus dealt with familiar terrain and people, and were able to avail themselves of the tribal structure in upholding the law. Eight additional police stations and posts, under the central headquarters in Beersheba, were put into operation: ʾAsluj, ʿAuja al-Hafir, Kurnub, Ras Zuweira, Wadi Ghamr, Umm Rashrash, al-ʿImara, and Jammama.

According to the description left by al-'Aref, such was the situation as of 1934. Subsequently, the status of the subsidiary police stations was enhanced and the deployment of the force began to move southwards into the heart of the Negev, according to a map by Bresslavsky (1946). Additional stations were also added, among them Quseima, Khalassa, ʿAyn Hasb (Husub), ʿAyn Ghadhyan, and Tall al-Melh (al-Malah).

The Bedouin considered their inclusion in the governmental structure a great honour. Each station was under the command of a Bedouin corporal or sergeant (*shawish*), usually from the family of a sheikh, and under him there were some ten men who would patrol the area. In 1934, the police force numbered 140 men, of whom 72 rode camels and 24 horses; 18 were foot soldiers. It should be noted that not all of the policemen were Bedouin (al-'Aref 1934: 280-81).

The author found another group of Bedouin who served as a police constable in the police station and security forces—Palestine Police Force—were: Mhammad Hasan Abu-Rabi'a (Police No. 2126), Sliman Sbayyih Abu-Rabi'a (as a wire-less operator, Police No. 1007) and his brother Salameh Sbayyih Abu-Rabi'a (Police No. 2622), Dib Salem Abu-Rabi'a (Police No. 1751) and his brother Hammad Salem Abu-Rabi'a (Police No. 1388), 'Ali Salman Abu-Rabi'a (Police No. 2603) and his brother Sliman Salman Abu-Rabi'a (Police No. 3029), 'Awda 'Iyd Abu-Rabi'a (*buliss hajjaneh*, Police No. 659), Khadder Khalil Abu-Rabi'a (Police No. 2031), Mhammad Hamad al-'Aqayly (Police No. 2029), Ibrahim Abu-Irqaiyiq, Salman al-'Atawna, Hammad al-Sane', Salameh Salman al-Huzaiyil. Some of the al-Wuhaydat of Tarabin, who used to live east of Gaza, served in the police and even achieved the rank of officer. The son of Sheikh Hasan al-Wuheidy served as a wireless operator in the police, then an official in the Qaimaqam office, and in the regional police office (Abu-Khusa 1994: 274-286; Bar-Zvi 1973: 26-32; Bar-Zvi 1977; Bresslavsky 1946: 255).

Al-'Aref (1934: 270) writes of the wireless and telephone connections between the stations and headquarters in Beersheba. All the stations had wireless but al-'Imara had a telephone; al-Jammama had no wireless, and no telephone.

It should be noted that the British authorities constructed fifty-four police stations in Palestine in the period from 1936 to 1939, as part of a construction programme aimed at establishing facts on the ground, both politically and in the sphere of security. Establishment of the police stations was one of the major construction projects in Mandatory Palestine in the 1930s. Situated on major transportation arteries or on high ground, and affording control of the surrounding area, these stations were built under the supervision of a retired police officer, Sir Charles Tegart (1881-1946), and bear his name. The Tegart- type police building in Beersheba was built between 1939 and 1942. Its north-eastern wing included the Ottoman Saraya, and its south-western included the gaol and police station from the Ottoman period. The structures that housed the Ottoman post office and wireless station remained outside the building.

The best trackers (*Qassassin*) in the government service were recruited from the Bedouin tribes. From footprints in the sand, they were able to glean such critical information as how many camels were in a convoy, when a convoy passed, the ages of the camels, whether they were lightly or heavily laden, how many riders were on the animals, and how many men or women traveled on foot (al-'Aref 1944: 29; Salameh Sbayyih Abu-Rabi'a, personal communication, 28 March, 1983).

Some of the famous trackers among the Bedouin tribes in the 30s were: 'Awadd Abu-Irqaiyiq, from Qudeirat; Nasser Abu-Nghaymesh, from Mhemdiyin of 'Azazma; Salem al-Zurei'y, from Ghawaly Tarabin; and Hassan Abu-Zaytun, from Jubarat. Sliman Abu- Nghaymesh, from Subhiyin of 'Azazma, could distinguish the footsteps of male wolves from she-wolves, and male camels from she-camels. Hassan Abu-Zaytun could distinguish the footprints of pregnant from non-pregnant women, and men's footprints from women's. The footprints of pregnant women are more stressed on the ground than those of non-pregnant women. The footprints of a man are larger than those of a woman. Other signs of differentiation between the sexes include differences in their gait. While a man tends to walk straight, that is, the sole of his foot is relatively straight, the gait of a woman is different. The angle of her foot is greater, she walks with her feet spread further apart, and the soles of her feet, especially around her toes, tend to the side, outward, more than do her heels. Another way to identify the sex of an intruder or someone walking in an unpaved area is by the way he or she urinates. A woman squats and spreads her legs, so that her urine is relatively close to her footprints and is spatially concentrated. A man is likely to pass his urine standing or squatting, and his urine lands somewhat further away and scatters especially if there is a wind.

The trackers distinguish the footprints of the male camel from the she-camel: the heel of a male camel hardly touches the ground, while that of a she-camel smoothly touches the ground; the male camel directs his urine to the back, but the she-camel directs hers on to her legs, although if she is pregnant, her urine spreads on her tail. The male wolf can be told from she-wolf: the paw and heel of the she-wolf are smaller than the wolf's; when the she-wolf urinates, she opens her back legs, but the wolf raises his leg when he urinates (Abu-Khusa 1994: 92, 225-226; Havakook 1998).

In the tents of the Bedouin, one can hear different versions of the following story. Two Bedouin men had an argument about which of them was the father of a ten-year-old boy. One, an elderly man, claimed that his wife had been in early pregnancy when he divorced her, she was in early pregnancy, and that when she remarried some months later, to the younger man, she gave birth to *his* son. The younger man insisted that when he married the woman, she was not pregnant; it was he who had impregnated her, and the boy was hence his son. The woman, who could have decided the matter with one short utterance, chose to remain silent. This being the case, with the woman absolutely refusing to tell her version of events, the two adversaries decided to take the matter to the Qadi, the traditional Bedouin judge, for a decision. The judge listened to the elderly man tell his side of the story, and then asked the young man to tell his. He then rubbed his forehead a bit, took one or two puffs on his pipe, and called the boy in 'Son, go to the field on the other side of the mountain, where a shepherdess is tending a flock, and bring me a sheep. But be careful not to let the shepherdess see you!'. The lad went to the field, and after a long time eventually returned with a lamb. The judge slaughtered the lamb and prepared for all present a Bedouin meal worthy of the name. The judge's guests, including the two adversaries, sat around the large bowls licking their fingers in delight. Towards evening, the shepherdess, who happened to be the *qadi*'s daughter, returned home. 'Father!' she unceremoniously addressed her father as she entered, oblivious to the others present. 'A lamb is missing. It was stolen! I checked the meadow and followed the signs on the ground until I ended up right here. The thief is here, among your guests!', 'And who do you think stole the lamb from your flock?' her father demanded. 'The thief is a young boy, a lad, whose father is old and mother young,' the shepherdess replied decisively. 'And on what basis do you state that the thief is a lad whose father is old and mother young?' the judge asked his daughter. 'On the basis of what he did, and especially on the basis of the signs he left on the ground.' 'Perhaps you'll explain what you mean,' the judge demanded of his daughter. 'Sometimes the boy carried the lamb on his shoulders, and sometimes he took it down, held it by the forelegs and pulled it from behind him,' She explained without hesitation. 'And what does it mean that sometimes he carried the lamb on his shoulders and sometimes took it down and dragged it from behind him?' 'When he had the strength of his young mother, he carried the lamb on his shoulders; when he was tired, like his old father, he took the lamb down and held it by its forelegs, and pulled it from behind him.' The judge eyed his guests and without hesitation, said: 'See, my daughter the shep-herdess has solved the problem you presented me with: The father of the boy is the old man!' (Havakook 1998: 149-150).

The British authorities built a customs house at the intersection of the roads leading to 'Auja al-Hafir and Kurnub. 'Auja located 77 km south-west of Beersheba; Kurnub located 40 km south-east of Beersheba. These roads were leading to the same place intersect. It was here that goods from the Sinai and Trans-Jordan were checked. Commencing in 1929, Bedouin who wished to enter Beersheba had to deposit their firearms at the customs house.

Al-'Aref (1934: 282) mentions the following names of customs officials:

1. Messbah effendi al-Nadher
2. Yusuf effendi Hamu
3. Rawak effendi Sabila
4. Fawzy effendi Farah

In 1923, the British placed a statue of General Allenby in the small Ottoman garden near the Saraya. The statue faced north, to commemorate the British advance in World War I through Palestine from south to north. The statue was demolished in 1938, during the rebellion headed by Abd al-Halim al-Julany, and was replaced by a stone column on a square base.

During the British Mandate, the city was able to boast a num-ber of especially comely residences. One of these was the residence of the Qaimaqam, built by Governor 'Aref al-'Aref. It was a large building with a colonnade along a courtyard that stretched along approximately a quarter of its circumference.

In 1918, the residential tent area of Beersheba was approxi-mately 20 acres (85 dunams). By 1935, the figure had risen to approximately 40 acres, and by 1947 to some 70 acres. The sharp increase between the latter two dates reflects the migration of Bedouin, as well as villagers and city people, to Beersheba during World War II (Ettingon 1979: 70-75).

British Authorities kept good relations with the Bedouin. The authority of the Qada governor to uphold the law was derived from Bedouin Control Ordinance No. 18, enacted on 7 May 1942 and amended in 1945. The ordinance empowered the governor to inves-tigate any disturbance and assault, arrest the guilty, and attach/foreclose their property. The provisions of the above ordinance were based on Bedouin custom, which recognised the responsibility of the *khams*, blood relatives through the fifth generation, for an individual's behaviour; authorised parties were allowed to arrest one of the transgressor's relatives, through the fifth degree, as a hostage in the event that the man himself had fled. In general, the cohesive group, khams, is the group that is liable to work together. This is composed of relatives who are related patrilinially to a common forefather, who 'lived five generations ago'. All the members participate in the cohesive group, although they may be more than five generations removed from that common ancestor. The cohesive group protect their members from attacks and extend help to them in different areas, for example defending the tribal territory (*dira*), mainly land and pasture fields, cisterns and wells. The main task of the khams is to share responsibility for 'blood'(*bihuttu fi al-ddamm*). In the event of a member of the group shedding blood, all members share in the payment of blood money (*diyih*). If one of them is killed or injured, all of them have to avenge his blood (Abu-Rabi'a 1994: 22; Ginat 1984: 59-82; Marx 1967: 58-60; al-'Aref 1933, 77-106).

The government's prerogatives included the appointment of sheikhs and the supervision of their activities. During the Mandate, the responsibilities of the sheikh towards the authorities included maintenance of security and preservation of order, and the regular collection of taxes.

The sheikh in the Negev, during the British Mandate, basically performed the functions of a government *Mukhtar* (village chief) in Arab villages, in addition to those of a government official (Shimoni 1947: 138,148; see also The Prevention of Inter Tribal and Factional Crimes Ordinance 1935: 557). The sheikhs would receive a payment (*Ikramiya*) from the government at the rate of 6 per cent of the taxes they collected, which proved an effective incentive in raising revenues from the tribes. The sheikh also received, or rather demanded, a fee (*Ujra*) from his tribe, at a rate agreed upon between himself and the tribe, of which the government was aware (al-'Aref 1933: 42). The ujra could be either in money or money equivalents, such as clarified butter, dried cheese, wheat or barley, sheep, goats, camels, horses, plots of land, etc. The Bedouin term for such payments was *massruf*, i.e., pocket money for expenses the sheikh would incur in the course of dealing with the affairs of the tribe.

They termed payment in commodities *musa'ada*, or participation in the sheikh's expenses and the cost of entertaining his guests. As of the end of 1931, the population of Beersheba was 2,959, of whom 135 were Bedouin (Government of Palestine 1946, I: 150). The very fact of residence in a city influenced a Bedouin's way of life and outlook, especially concerning education, which had considerable influence on the sheikhs and their sons. An example of a sheikh who was aware of the importance of schooling and higher education was sheikh 'Ali al-'Atawna, of Beersheba, who gave his children an education, especially his sons Farid and Selim. Farid was appointed a Treasury official in Beersheba; after the 1948 war between Israel and Arabs in Palestine, he immigrated to Kuwait. There, his son 'Ali became manager of Sabah Hospital; another son, Kamal, became a teacher. Sheikh 'Ali's son Selim completed the Kadoori (Khadouri) Agricultural School in Tul-Karm, and was appointed agricultural supervisor for the Beersheba district. After the 1948 war, he was expelled to Hebron and served in the Jordanian army (al-'Aref 1934: 113-14; Bresslavsky 1946: 251; Erskine 1935: 203; Gal-Pe'er 1979a: 281-82, 296).

For the semi-nomadic Palestine Bedouin in the 1930s, there was a serious lack of educational facilities. For instance, only five schools existed in Beersheba, serving a population of a hundred thousand in the surrounding district. An itinerant school for those who lived far from any settled area would have been a step in the right direction. Many of the tent-dwelling Bedouin went to school to be able to read the Quran (Erskine, 1935:198-21).

Most of the mayors of Beersheba during the Mandatory period were Bedouin. Sheikh 'Ali al-'Atawna was mayor until his death in 1922, when the British appointed Sheikh Hmeid al-Sufy. Al-Sufy served a brief tenure, and was succeeded by Sheikh Freih Abu-Meddein, who served for a year or two. His successor, Sheikh Hajj Hsein Abu-Kaff, went on to serve a long tenure, eventually being succeeded by the city secretary, Abu-'Atef, who was of Hebron lineage. Abu-'Atef was succeeded by Taj al-Din Sha'th, of Gaza lineage, who became the first elected mayor in the city's history. In 1946, Shafiq Mushtaha, a non-Bedouin, was elected mayor, and Sheikh Salameh Ibn-Sa'id, deputy mayor (Bar-Zvi 1977).

The actual number of Negev Bedouin in Mandatory Palestine is subject to dispute. The 1932 census had counted some 40,000 Bedouin, but al-'Aref (1934) puts the actual number in the range of

75,000-100,000. Shim'oni (1947: 148) puts their number in the range of 50,000-60,000, on the basis of computations performed during World War II. According to Muhsam (1966: 23), there were about 65,000 Negev Bedouin at the end of the British Mandate.

In 1945, Beersheba had a population of 5,570, of whom 5,360 were Muslim, 200 Christian, and 10 'other' (al-Dabbagh, 1991:352). During the preceding years the population of Beersheba, according to al-Dabbagh (1991: 351-52), was as follows:

Table 3.1   Population of Beersheba 1902-1945

Year	Muslim	Christian	Jew	Druze	Other	Total
1902						300
1912						800
1915						1000
1922	2012	235	98	11	—	2356
1931	2791	152	11	—	5 Bahais	2959*
1945	5360	200	—	—	10	5570**

*   1568 men and 1391 women.

** Most of the population was of Gaza or Hebron origin, with a minority of Bedouin.

The Beersheba city limits contained 3,890 dunams, of which 464 were roads and approximately 80 dunams of Jewish-owned land.[464 and 80 are part of the 3,890]

In 1946, the total population of Beersheba was 6,490, all of them Arab (Anglo-American Committee for inquiry, 1946: 151, Table 8b). Marx (1967: 34-36) notes that during the thirty years of British rule, all Beersheba Qaimaqams were Arab, none Bedouin. These officials, though, were close to the Bedouin, understood their needs and forged personal links with the sheikhs. The governor would meet sheikhs, not only when in Beersheba to attend to tribal affairs or for sessions of the Tribal Court, but also at their reception tents, which enhanced their standing with their own people. The sheikhs received salaries, although not large ones, for the services they rendered the authorities.

The Bedouin remember the period of the British Mandate fondly, often entertaining nostalgic feelings for it. Marx (1967: 10) writes of an elderly Bedouin who told him that the 'British were good to us; they are the best rulers in the world. They always stood by their word and we were free to do as we pleased, except fight each other. At that time, the whole country was ours, and no one required permits to work, for weapons, or even to sell animals.'

Many of the British were attracted to the Bedouin and tried to become close to them, such as the last governor of the Qada, the Lord of Oxford and Asquith. British sympathy and tolerance for the Bedouin, in comparison to the Ottomans, made them very popular. A boarding school for Bedouin children was established in Beersheba, mainly for the sons of sheikhs. The authorities hoped to train future leaders who would cultivate the personal qualities required for contact with government officialdom. Thus the Bedouin were brought within the purview of the government's authority, but could do as they pleased in all spheres. Only in emergencies did the British extend the Bedouin generous assistance. For example, during the drought of 1927, the authorities had helped find new pasture lands for Bedouin flocks, and from 1942 to 1945 the British provided the Bedouin with work outside tribal areas, building military bases and airfields in the Negev.

During World War II, the British authorities would distribute regulated commodities such as sugar, coffee, sardines, powdered eggs, and butter to the residents of Beersheba and Bedouin in the surrounding area (Ettingon 1979: 70). The British Military's heavy demand for food, especially beer, for which the barley grown by the Bedouin was the main raw material, caused a rise in the prices of some commodities produced by the Bedouin. Beersheba became a central market for barley and mutton for the military in World War II; trade in sheep and supply thereof to government purchasers engaged the entire Bedouin population of the Negev, as well as that of the Sinai, Trans-Jordan, and the Hejaz (Bresslavsky 1946: 254). Nevertheless, the whole of the Negev was also used for raising other livestock. Some of the sheikhs and notables became contractors for the supply of commodities, such as mutton for the British forces. A firm, Steel Brothers, acted as the intermediary between the British Army and the sheikhs. The Bedouin thought of Steel Brothers as a 'governmental agency'. Many Bedouin would bring their sheep and goats from the Sinai Peninsula, from Trans-Jordan, Iraq, and even the Hejaz, in the Arabian Peninsula. Some sheikhs united to supply sheep and excess grain to the 'government agency'. It should be noted that sheep had been imported from Trans-Jordan and Iraq during the nineteen and twenty centuries (Abu-Rabia 1994a:13; Avitsur 1976: 46). Beersheba, Gaza and Khan Yunis served as a centres for buying and selling Bedouin barley and other cereals. Other locations in the Negev served as intermediate centres for collecting livestock, wool, camels, livestock droppings and manure, and skins, to send them to the main commercial centres (Bresslavsky 1946: 254).

It should be noted that cattle and livestock manure used to be a main source of energy and heating in Middle Eastern countries, including Palestine (Avitsur 1976: 61; Miller 1996: 521-28; Nesbitt 1995: 68-81). Even in the 1990s, there is widespread use of live-stock and cattle droppings and manure in the Negev, mainly for heating and preparing food, tea, coffee, and boiling water for cleansing purposes. The Bedouin store dried manure in piles for more than one year. The gathering and storing is the women's duty. Some of the settled Bedouin, of peasant (*fallahin*) origin, still use the *tabun* to bake bread. 'The *Tabun* made of mud and hay. The *tabun* is an separate room whose ground is laid with pebbles (*radhaff*), the poker used is called *muqhar*. Some burning coals is placed among the manure that fills it to distribute the heat. This raises the temperature sufficiently to bake dozens of loaves for the many families that share it' (Jordan Museum of Popular Traditions at Amman, 1998). According to Avitsur (1976: 242-43) the Bedouin would burn thorny shrubs for fuel, especially Poterium spinosum (*bellan, natsh*), widely prevalent in rocky and hilly areas. Among other advantages, these shrubs are dry and give off considerable heat.

The site on which the city of Beersheba was built had been a meeting place where Jewish traders would pitch tents and conduct business with the Bedouin. The British would transact with the Bedouin to buy barley which was in demand among distillers in Scotland, and poison hemlock (Conium maculatum L.: *shawkaran*) for the pharmaceutical industry in Hamburg. The goods would be shipped to Europe via Gaza (Weitz 1947: 139-50). Such commerce continued during the British Mandate, with the centre for the procurement of commodities in Beersheba (Gal-Pe'er 1979b: 83-100).

The biggest change in the Bedouin way of life during the Mandate occurred in the sphere of economics, in which Beersheba played an important role, both directly and indirectly. As an urban centre, Beersheba was a source of the goods the Bedouin needed, and also a market where they could sell their produce. Beersheba's shops were full of sheep's wool, goat's hair, coils of palm fibre for the manufacture of ropes, thick cords and mats, ropes for drawing water, and nets for tying hay and grains into bundles on camels' backs. On Wednesday market days, the city would come to life, the number of people in its streets doubling. The Bedouin would throng the city's thoroughfares and crowd its coffee shops. They would stable their camels and horses at khans especially established for that purpose at the entrance to the city. For a fee a groom would water and feed the animals and watch them until their owners returned. The khans in Beersheba were: al-Far, Abu-Jrir, Jauhar, and al-Baladiya (Bar-Zvi 1977).

The Bedouin spent market day trading in livestock and other commodities, drinking coffee, and smoking hookahs. For the Bedouin, market day was an opportunity for socialising and maintaining inter-tribal contacts, for sheikhs to meet each other, for ironing out differences between and within tribes, and for maintaining pan-tribal social connections.

At the market, the Bedouin would buy tea, coffee, sugar, cloth-ing, spices, firearms, cooking utensils, agricultural tools, saddles, porcelain vases, dry goods, gold and silver jewellery, tobacco (both domestic and imported), brass trays, daggers (*shabary*, sing. *she-briya*), leather belts, and signature seals—mainly for sheikhs. The Bedouin, both men and women, would sell camels, horses, don-keys, sheep, goats, mules, tent flaps of goat hair, goat hair, woolen rugs, sheepskins, dried cheeses, clarified butter, barley, wheat, med-icinal herbs, fowl, eggs, fermented milk, and braiding.

Usually, the Bedouin women stored the dried cheeses (*'afig*) in jute or cotton sacks, so they could have enough ventilation. 'Afig must be very dry before storing. They stored clarified butter (*samen*) in clay jars (*jarrah*) or special skins called *'ukkah*, which were also used to store samen and olive oil. Their volume would be between 15 and 25 litres. The jars were sealed with smooth, flat stones smeared with mud mixed with straw. Bedouin who lived near caves stored the jars there, so as not to have to take them during the wan-dering season (*'izbeh*). In the Negev there are a lot of broken jars (*fukhkhar, qarqum ibriq*). Some Bedouin store samen in tins, but only for short periods.

According to Avitzur (1976: 240, 271-79), largescale manufac-ture of earthenware vessels took place at a number of renowned centres, the most noted of which, in both quality and production volume, was at the time, and remains, the city of Gaza. Firing was performed in small, two-level kilns. On the lower level, a fire was kept stoked, while on the upper level, a perforated mud sheet was spread on which the clay vessels would be baked. In the north and centre of the country, wood, especially oak root, was the main fire fuel, while in Gaza, which has no trees, hay was used. Firing would last up to six days. In household pottery works kept by women, clay vessels were fired in holes dug in the ground, with dry dung serving as the main fuel. In the north of the country, most pottery was yellowish brown, while in the south, vessels were mostly black. The black colour was attained by smoking the pottery: at the end of the baking process, moist dung would be burnt, emitting a smoke so thick it would clog the ventilation and engulf the pottery.

Pottery was traditionally inexpensive. During the British Mandate, large, high-quality earthenware vessels could be obtained for a *grush*, and small vessels could be purchased for a *ta'rifa* (half a grush). They were sold both at openair markets (*souqs*) and by vendors who brought pottery direct to the villages. Even when an earthenware vessel was broken, it would not be discarded. The broken fragments would be pounded into powder with a rolling pin or pestle. The powder was important in plastering structures, especially cisterns.

The Bedouin also used lime (*shid*) for plastering their cisterns. Lime was used in construction and masonry with cement, in whitewashing, and in soap production. Lime was is derived from chalk by burning. This would be done in simple kilns in close proximity to where the chalk was found. Lime kilns were made by digging a round hole three metres wide, two and a half metres deep. After the hole was dug, the chalk and fuel for a fire would be brought to it. Stones of chalk would be arranged in a circular dome in the pit. The burning process would last three to six days, without letup. After the burning was finished, the kiln would be left to cool for four to six days. The lime would then be taken out. The large lime blocks along the edge of the pit were considered of the highest quality, while the small pieces towards the centre of the pit were considered grade B. One camel load, or *cantur* (*qentar/quntar* = 100 *ratels*, or 250-300 kilogram), of lime would fetch 40 grush on the Jerusalem market in the early 1880s.

More sophisticated kilns, in permanent structures, were first constructed in the early years of the twentieth century. Modern kilns in the full sense of the term made their first appearance in Palestine during the British Mandate. Kiln workers tended to be concerned for their eyes, and after a shift would sprinkle *kohl* on them or put some drops of oil of black cumin (Nigella sativa: *habbet al-baraka*). Lime was also used in one of the more common methods of fishing in Palestine during the nineteenth century. Lime, mixed with a medicinal powder of storax (Styrax officinalis: *luban*), or the bulb of Aleppo cyclamen (Cyclamen persicum Mill.: *sabunet al-ra'y*), would be sprinkled over water. These poisonous mixtures would stun fish, which would then come to the surface and be collected by the fishermen. Such methods, as well as fishing with explosives, which came into use early in the twentieth century, were banned by the British Mandatory authorities.

According to Doumani (1995: 122, 187) and al-Nimr (1961: 288-89), the alkali (*qelw*) used in soapmaking in Nablus was imported from Bedouin lands on the east bank of the River Jordan, during the last centuries (1700-1900). Cohen (1989: 81-85) and Ze'evi (1996:106) describe the process of soapmaking during the sixteenth and seventeenth centuries in Ottoman Jerusalem. Burckhard (1822: 354-55) witnessed this process in 1812. The Bedouin gathered barilla plants (saltwort: Salsola kali—*hurd* ;and Salsola soda—*Shawk ahmar*) in huge quantities, burned it, and transported the ashes to Nablus in large caravans. Until the introduction of caustic soda in the 1860s, Bedouin from the Bani-Sakhr, Huwaittat, and 'Adwan tribes gathered barilla in the valley of M'an, around Salt and Tadmor (Palmyra). Among the Bedouin of Syrian desert and Saudia Arabia, another saltwort (Seidlitzia rosmarinus: *shenan, ishnan, ushnan, duwwayd*) is used for cleaning as a soap substitute, and is traded for grains such as wheat and barley (Jabbur 1995: 64-81; Dickson 1955:86; Musil 1928a:134).

The rug and wool industries were central to the Bedouin economy. In the 1920s textile dye works were established in Beersheba (Bresslavsky 1946: 242; Ettingon 1979: 69-80; Gal-Pe'er 1979a: 282; Kressel and Ben-David 1995: 119-44). It should be noted that Hebron, Gaza, and Majdal were famous for their dye-works. The most prevalent colour was blue, which was extracted from indigo (*nileh*) plants, both local and imported, mainly from India. From the beginning of the nineteenth century until the end of Egyptian rule in 1840, trade in indigo was a monopoly. The colour red was extracted from plants of the madder (Rubia: *fouwwa*) family, which grow in Palestine, as well as safflower (Carthamus tinctorius: *'usfur, qurtum*). It was also extracted from local scarlet (*qermez, qurmez*) and oak worms. The colours black and brown were extracted from pomegranate and onion peels. Yellowish-green was extracted from tamarisk (Tamarix spp.: *ithl, ithil*) and rhus (*summaq*). Alum was used as a colour stabiliser, as were lemons, unripe grapes, and a mixture of honey, grapes, lime, and the ash of kili and other plants (Avitzur 1976: 268).

Among the Bedouin of the Negev, substances derived from plants such as the rhus, pomegranate (*rumman*), and Pistacia palaestina (*butum*) are used in the tanning of skins (Abu-Rabi'a 1999b). The Bedouin of the Syrian desert, used the rind of the pomegranate for dyeing and tanning; the leaves, pods and bark of acacia (*salama*, pl. *salam*) were also used for tanning hides. The leaves of the *basham*a bush (apparently, Commiphora obobalsamum: Balm of Gilead; Balsam of Mecca would be *balasan, balsam Makka*. The author's interpretations were used to blacken the hair; it was dried, pounded into a powder, soaked in water, and mixed with henna (Lawsonia inermis: *henna*). Another plant used was saltwort (Seidlitzia rosmarinus). Saltwort turns yellowish when it dries, and clothes washed in it acquire a tinge of this yellow hue (Jabbur 1995: 64-81). Through the ages, natural plants dyes have been used in Palestine (Sorek and Ayalon 1993).

In the early years of the mandate, the British forbade the growing of Bedouin tobacco (*hishiy*), except in a specified area of the Negev. The Bedouin were highly fond of that variety, preferring it to all others. Thus, the British announcement on 21 September 1933 that the partial ban was being repealed, and that the cultivation of hishiy would be permitted throughout the province, was on occasion for rejoicing (al-'Aref 1934: 271). According to Avitsur (1976:105, 198-99), most time spent in coffee houses in nineteenth-century Palestine was passed in smoking narghiles. For half a grush, a customer would get a smoking piece with enough tobacco (Nicotiana glauca: *tumbak*) for several hours. Tobacco was grown in the country on a small scale, and much of the imported supply was smuggled. In the last quarter of the nineteenth century, raising and selling tobacco had been subject to regulation and tax by the Ottoman authorities. Small quantities of simple tobacco were grown in the northern Negev. In World War I, with the cessation of imports from Iran, cultivation areas expanded considerably.

In the Mandatory Palestine, the British founded agricultural-educational institutions and introduced a aforestry policy (El-Eini,

1999a, 1999b). A special effort was made to expand agriculture in the Negev. Experimental agricultural stations and a fowl-breeding station were established. Large-scale tree planting was undertaken, for both shade and beauty. One of the agricultural supervisors (in 1933) was Muhammad effendi al-Sharif (Gal-Pe'er 1991a: 15).

The British authorities did much to keep track of the development of Beersheba, by conducting censuses and surveys. It was in fact the British who introduced the use of statistical measurements, censuses, and tax assessment surveys in the city, as well as modern map-making (Tal 1991:52).

Al-'Aref (1934: 272) notes that after the World War I, there was a decline in the raising of camels, horses, and sheep. Furthermore, the value of camels and horses declined, because of the automobile. A drop in the value of sheep and sheep products on the Beersheba market, a government proscription of trade in salt and firearms, a ban on burning firewood, and a complete ban on the raid (*ghazu*) all contributed towards the Bedouins' increased dependence on the authorities, and of the city's people on the Beersheba administration. During the drought of 1927, the government transported, at its own expense, the Bedouin and their livestock to the Bisan Valley. In rainy years the government would extend agricultural loans and give tax benefits to ease the economic transition the Bedouin were undergoing. The early 1930s were a time of economic depression. At one point, the Qaimaqam, al-'Aref could not find a single Bedouin in his district who was not in debt, to some extent or other, to either the government or traders. One of the taxes of the period was the *daribat al-ta'dad* (counting tax), of 48 mils per head of sheep and 120 mils per camel. Unscrupulous traders from outside the area took advantage of the distress of the Bedouin, and began to acquire plots of land from them.

In 1934, there were seven orchards in Beersheba, a club for government officials, parks, and schools for both boys and girls, including a boarding school for Bedouin boys. The city had three water wells. Beersheba had two mosques, one built in Ottoman times, and the other in 1931, by the generosity of Hajj 'Isa Bsisu. According to Tal (1991: 49-50), there were two churches in Beersheba: one Protestant, built around 1910 by American missionaries, and one Greek Orthodox. The Protestant church operated a Sunday school. World War II brought about an economic recovery for the Bedouin, and many of them even became wealthy. The British augmented their military presence in the Negev during the war. The Beersheba-'Auja axis, which contained the two main roads to Beersheba, those from Gaza and Hebron, was one of the two main supply axis to the Suez Canal and Egypt. Military bases were built in the vicinity of Beersheba, as was an airfield north-west of the city. A military base was also built in Bir-'Asluj.

The population of Beersheba grew in the war years, leading to increased demand for services. The growth of Beersheba's population and its prosperity had a direct impact on the standard of living of the Bedouin in the entire area. The rise in the Bedouin standard of living, in turn, had an impact on a number of social and economic spheres (al-'Aref 1934: 254-78; Bresslavsky 1946:253-56; Gal-Pe'er, 1979a: 283-84). The British employed Bedouin in the construction of roads and military bases, and bought Bedouin land for military use. Beersheba became a commercial centre. In addition to legitimate commerce, it was also a centre for trade in smuggled and stolen goods.

Beersheba also became a centre for medical services during the British Mandate. In the 1920s, the government-employed veterinary surgeon for the livestock market, Dr. Levi, also treated people on occasion, due to the lack of doctors in the city (Gal-Pe'er 1979b: 93). A quarantine on the livestock and cattle the Bedouin brought to sell was established near the market. It is worth noting that in the British Mandate, the condition of Bedouin agriculture, especially the raising of livestock, began to improve because of the inauguration of government veterinary services and the quarantine station, which helped to wipe out epidemics. In 1933, Mr 'Abd al-'Aziz effendi al-Massry was the quarantine officer. The Negev's veterinary service records from the Mandatory period show that livestock, cattle, fowls, dogs, cats, and other animals suffered from the following contagious and infectious diseases of animals: sheep and goat pox (jadra), fowl pox, fowl typhoid (tifuid), fowl plague (ta'un), fowl cholera (kolira), epizootic lymphangitis (limfawy), rabies (s'ar), mange (jarab), scabies (gharab), anthrax (jamra), strongylosis (j'am dud), dourine (bajal), foot and mouth disease (shqaq, humma qula'iya), piroplasmosis (kumthariyat), glanders (sqaweh), tuberculosis (sell), sheep and goat scab (julba), sarcoptic (humak), African horse sickness (najma), parasitic gastroenteritis of sheep and goats (khrag).

The chief veterinary officer for the Negev in the period from 1925 to 1937, (and later the director of veterinary services in Palestine) was J. M. Smith. He was succeeded by G. B. Simmins, who served from1938 to 1947, who was succeeded by L. F. Robertson from December 1947 to January or February 1948. H. R. Binns was acting director of veterinary services during the 40s (Government of Palestine 1925-1948). Some of these diseases were treated by traditional Bedouin healers (Abu-Rabi'a 1999a).

At the end of the nineteenth century, there were some 35,000 donkeys in Palestine, 18,000 of them in the Jerusalem district. Prices for ordinary donkeys were in the range of 5-10 *majidi*. According to official Ottoman government statistics, there were some 15,000 camels, including Negev camels, in the southern part of the country and the Jerusalem district. In 1930, the camel population in all of Palestine was estimated at 25,000 (Avitsur 1976: 227). Abu-Khusa (1976-1979) claims that the flocks of the Bedouin in 1943 were numbered as follows: camels 13,784; sheep 70,000; cattle 90,500; domestic fowls 52,000. Bresslavsky (1946: 138) puts the number of camels in the 1940s at 15,000.

The number of livestock, cattle, and fowls among the Negev Bedouin in different years is shown in the following table:

Table 3.2   Negev Bedouin Livestock Populations, 1921-1943

	Horses	Mules	Donkeys	Camels	Cows	Sheep	Goats
1921	?	?	?	10,000	?	53,058	35,203 (al-'Aref, 1933:224-225)
1928	?	?	?	8,638	?	50,400	34,285 (Ibid.)
1932	?	?	?	16,979	?	61,676	43,588 (Ibid.)
1934	2,020	6	14,988	13,426	3,989	55,492	38,236 (Statis.Abst.Palst.1935)
1937	2,484	7	18,902	11,476	6,048	42,435	22,048 (Statis.Abst.Palst.1938)
1943	2,611	84	24,080	13,784*	9,946	26,079*	34,659* (Statis.Abst.Palst.1944/45)

* over one year old.
For more details, see Abu-Rabi'a 1994a.

Table 3.3   Negev Bedouin Fowl Populations, 1934-1943

	Chickens	Ducks	Geese	Turkeys	Pigeons	Total
1934	104,445	200	103	100	1,652	106,500 (Statis.Abst.Palst.1935)
1937	No specific breakdown					131,022 (Statis.Abst.Palst.1938)
1943	51,200	No specific breakdown				51,750 (Statis.Abst.Palst.1944/45)

For more details, see Abu-Rabi'a 1994a.

At the time of the British conquest of Beersheba, a single military hospital, situated in the Bedouin school building, served the entire Beersheba region. After World War I, it reverted to being a school. In the beginning of the Mandatory period, a government hospital was built in Beersheba. The city's health services included a government physician, Dr. Sulayman Selim al-Sama'yn, who was manager of the hospital. Dr. Khalil Abu-Ghazaleh served as a medical officer in Beersheba during the periods of 1921-23, and 1924-29; in the year of 1923-24 he served in Haifa (al-'Aref 1934: 55, 282; Cornfeld 1947: 5-6; Aurel and Cornfeld 1945: 10). A private physician, Dr. 'Abd al-Razzaq Qlibu (Kleibo), who also served as a Qaimaqam in 1926-27, practised in the city. In time, a Greek physician, Dr. Dimitriades, and several Jewish physicians took up residence in Beersheba. The Jewish physicians were Dr. Meir Berkovitz, who came to the city in the early 1920; and Dr. Reuben Meir, who practiced in 1935-36. A Jewish dentist, Dr. Rabinowitz, practiced in Beersheba, along with a Jewish woman dentist. The Jewish doctors treated Bedouins as well as city-dwellers. Since these were the only doctors in the entire district, the Bedouin had to bring even the seriously ill to Beersheba; thus Beersheba came to be identified in the Bedouin mind as a medical centre. The city's eight-bed hospital employed a doctor, pharmacist, three nurses, and several others, including several male nurses. One of them (in 1933) was Saber effendi Abu al-Khayr.

The hospital and its outpatient clinic treated some 200 people daily, and served as a medical centre for outlying clinics, located at 'Auja al-Hafir, al-'Imara, and al-Jammama, which the hospital's physician would visit from time to time. During al-'Aref's tenure as Qaimaqam (1929-1939), a district health officer with offices in Beersheba was appointed. He would visit encampments in outlying areas, and dispense medical aid and advice. One such health officers (in 1933) was Ibrahim effendi Abu-Ghazaleh. Al-'Aref notes that the tribes of the northern and western areas of the district, who were closer to urban centres, tended to have more faith in medicine and doctors than those in the eastern and southern areas. This became more pronounced in the 1930s, when the Bedouin came to have more faith in medicine, visited hospitals more frequently, and anxiously awaited doctor's visits to their encampments.

Beersheba also had a pharmacist, who had been in the city in the Ottoman period. The pharmacist was responsible for arranging medical examinations for the courts in cases of homicide and injuries sustained in clashes between Bedouin tribes. In 1933, there was a male nurse, Yusuf effendi al-'Isa (al-'Aref 1934: 269-83; Gal-Pe'er 1979a: 281-82, 1979b: 93). It worth noting that during that period, the Bedouin made use of their own traditional healers, including herbalists.

It should be noted that in the Beersheba area there are public water rights, such as those pertaining to treams and wadis, and private rights arising from the construction of water cisterns known as *harab* (sing. *haraba*). There are hundreds of harab, holes dug in the ground, plastered with mud, and protected against unlawful use by coverings of various kinds and degrees of security. Into these cisterns are trained streams of rainwater, which are reserved for summer use. The Bedouin are proud of their harab and even count their riches by their number. In addition to the harab, they build dams of stone, where it is possible to collect water and minimize erosion of lower-level land.

So scarce is water in the dry season that it is sometimes necessary for a man to set out at sunrise to reach a water cistern and return with drinking water for his household by nightfall.

There are 148 wells and hundreds of harab, but the cases can be numbered on the fingers. The Bedouin use goat- and sheepskin (*qerba*) for carrying water. The volume of a qerba is 25-40 litres. Women and girls carry the qerba on their backs with the help of rope on the forehead or on donkeys and camels, but not on horses.

Over his haraba the Bedouin exercises complete proprietorial rights. No one can dictate to him when he shall use the water or how, and with the exception of the passer by who wishes to slake his own thirst, no one dares touch the water without his permission. Permission to water animals is not freely given. There is always the danger that although dug by an individual, constant use by others over a period of time might establish a claim to have the haraba permanently available for general use. Every haraba must have its intake channel. This channel must not cross the land of a neighbour without agreement between the parties.

Generally speaking, running water in tribal areas is regarded as the property of the tribe. There are seven valleys (wadis) of considerable size in the Negev: Shallala, Shari'a, Meshash, Hasi, 'Asluj, 'Araba and Saba'. Each has a number of tributaries. With the exception of Hasi and Saba' wadis, the water is saline.

It should be noted that in the drought year of 1860, there were in the old city of Jerusalem 950 cisterns. The Muslim population had a 'grant' of one pitcher, later one tin (16 litres), per day for the needy, from the 34 big cisterns of the al-Aqsa (Avitur 1976: 43). In 1915, Beersheba had at least 15 wells, which supplied about 390,000 gallons of water per day (Pink 1991: 38-44). During the Mandate, the British Government made efforts to secure water supplies by drilling wells, but in every case it was found that where there was ample water it was of high salinity and where fresh water was found the flow was too slight to be of use (al-'Aref 1944: 184-86).

The owner of a cistern can sell the water to another Bedouin. Sometimes two or more Bedouin have a common right (*sherkeh*) on the water. The unit by which the water is used or sold is a classical Bedouin measurement called a *shebr* (the span of the hand, about 23 cm or 9 inches). This unit of length was practiced to measure a volume of water by using a rope of tent (*habl*).

No human can survive without water, so water resources are very important for the Bedouin in the desert. For example, in the year 1863 it was so dry that the Bedouin were compelled to abandon their areas in search of fodder for their animals and food for themselves. So near were they to famine that they had to eat animals that had died from thirst. That year was known as the Year of Animal Hides (*sanat al-jeldeh*). In 1874 drought forced all the tribes to migrate to Trans-Jordan. In 1927 the Palestine Government transported the Bedouin free of charge to Beisan. The year is known as *Sanat Beisan*.

The Palestine Government had come to the aid of the Bedouin in an earlier period after the British occupation by providing seed and fodder loans and writing off taxes due. Otherwise the tribes would have been in sorry plight indeed. The depression of 1931 onwards also had its repercussion on the tribes. Prices of products dropped and the Bedouin became indebted to the merchants in the villages. Camels fell in value. The concession to a company to transport the products of the Dead Sea deprived the Bedouin of his part in the salt trade. Whereas once he could obtain much grain for a load of salt, which cost him only the trouble of traveling hundreds of miles to Sodom for it and carrying it hundreds of miles to market, it henceforth became illegal to be found with a load of salt unless under license.

According to Avitzur (1976:278), salt is sacred in Bedouin tradition. It is considered a sacrilege to rob a salt carrier, or for one man to steal the salt of another. In 1862, salt became a monopoly of the Ottoman government, and the government leased a franchise on its importation. Local production and trade became clandestine. In 1881, revenues derived from salt passed from the government to the administration of the Ottoman public debt; Ottoman subjects could legally salt their food only after paying the salt tax. The Bedouin collectors and purveyors of salt began to smuggle it to the rural population, without worrying about the public debt. Well into the twentieth century, elderly Arab villagers would recall from childhood how masked Bedouin would appear at night and quickly sell salt to their fathers. Nevertheless, on the eve of World War I, most of Palestine's domestic salt requirements were imported through the port of Jaffa. Domestic salt trade came into the open after the British conquest. The tables then turned, and the axe came down on foreign salt. Along with firearms and hashish, the importation of salt was forbidden.

At 'Aqaba in 1931 there was a conference about raids. It was attended by a large number of sheikhs from Sinai, Trans-Jordan, and Palestine. Sinai Governor Jarvis Bey represented the Egyptian Government, Peak Pasha, the Officer Commanding the Arab Legion, represented Trans-Jordan, and 'Aref al-'Aref represented the Palestine Government. They succeeded in settling claims and blood feuds between the border tribes. The sheikhs enjoyed the conference and all looked pleased about things in general.

Part of the Bedouin economic structure was the trade in firearms. In the old days one rarely met a Bedouin who was not armed. The carrying of firearms was prohibited during the British Mandate except in a very limited area (al-'Aref 1934: 267-78; 1944: 184-86).

Firearms had appeared in Palestine in the sixteenth century, after the Ottoman conquest. However, in everyday use, firearms only made their appearance in the country some two centuries later, in the second half of the eighteenth century. The firearms in use in Palestine at the time were those usual for the period: barrel-loaded, with flint ignition for the gunpowder. Ammunition was ordinarily prepared at home. Imported lead would be cast into bullets, or into fragmentation clusters in special stone moulds. Gunpowder was manufactured from locally produced sulphur, wood coal, and salt-petre. The sulphur would be collected in the Judaean Desert, near the Dead Sea. Wood coal was obtained wherever there were natural tree groves, and the saltpetre would be made from goat dung. The dung would be scraped, steeped in water, and boiled. Afterwards, it would be strained through a cloth, which would trap the pieces of dung. The saltpetre solution would pass through, and be reheated. After drying in the sun, the sediment would be pounded and strained again.

Gunpowder was manufactured in commercial quantities in localities where sulphur deposits were prevalent, such as Bayt Jubrin and the surrounding area, as well as in the vicinity of Bedouin tribes in the Judaean Desert. The main use of sulphur was in the production of gunpowder; however, it was also used to fumigate rooms against insects, sterilise utensils, and treat livestock. The manufacture of gunpowder continued into the early years of the twentieth century, and was never fully discontinued even during the British Mandate. The gunpowder was used for both hunting and construction work, especially in blasting quarry stones. Gunpowder was stored in horns. In the more distant past, these were actually animal horns, but in time they were replaced by tin receptacles. Gourds (*qara'*), which are impervious to water and mildew, were commonly used as recently as the early twentieth century. In fact, so prevalent was the use of gourds to store gunpowder that when they were eventually replaced by bronze receptacles, the latter were called 'gourds' (Avitsur 1976: 274-77).

Asphalt was used to seal cracks and make medicines; another possible use was in the making of dye and paint. Eventually, increased demand, particularly after the British came, gave rise to the need for the production of much larger quantities, and from cheaper sources. These needs were met by asphalt produced in the mines of Hatzbaya, Lebanon, from which the material was also exported overseas (Avitsur 1976: 274-77).

It should be noted that natural asphalts were widely used in the ancient world, as far back as about 9000 B.C. Asphalt was commonly used in ancient Mesopotamia in building materials such as mortar and cement, paving for roads, waterproof pipes, insecticides, as well as for making fire; and for medical uses and magic rituals. Dead Sea bitumen was ingredient of balms in Egyptian mummies (Connan, Nissenbaum, and Dessort 1992: 2,743-59; Nissenbaum 1978: 837-44).

According to Bedouin sources (Hajj Hammad Salem abu-Rabi'a, personal communication, 21 August, 1998), the Bedouin called the asphalt *hummarah*. Asphalt, which is congealed petroleum, would be collected by the Bedouin at least once a year, in the form of blocks floating on the Dead Sea. The petroleum would flow into the Dead Sea with springs or ground water, and then congeal into bright reddish-black blocks with a pleasant odour. An easterly wind would blow the asphalt blocks towards the western shore. The Bedouin would break the large blocks into smaller blocks that could be loaded onto camels. They would sell these blocks to Arab traders in Hebron, Jerusalem, and elsewhere. In Palestine, very small quantities of asphalt were so collected, a fact reflected in its price: in 1872, a camel-load of asphalt fetched 500 grush in Jerusalem and Bethlehem. Such trade was an important source of income for the Bedouin tribes that controlled the western shore of the Dead Sea.

The Bedouin would make tar pastes out of the asphalt, which would be spread on tree and vine stumps after pruning as well as on cracks in pottery. It would be boiled in olive oil over a flame and chewed like gum. Medicines were also made out of the asphalt for dental therapy. It would also be used to hold the jaws or to treat inflammation of the gums, and to treat children's stuttering, by freeing their tongue so they could speak more easily, to treat fever, diarrhoea, and inflammation of the uterus. Asphalt was also used to treat skin diseases in animals and humans being. According to Brewer and Teeter (1999: 5) "In the seventeenth century eating dried flesh of a mummified corpse was considered a medical cure-all. The flesh and wrapping of Egyptians mummies were covered with a dark resinous substance, likened to bitumen, and were therefore referred to as mummy".

In contrast to meagre asphalt production, larger quantities of oil were produced from 'Moses rocks' (*ihjar Musa*), the oil-bearing bituminous shale rocks found in the locality of the large building on the traditional burial place of Moses, near Jericho. The Bedouin, who maintain ritual visits to Moses' tomb, believe that God blessed the place where Moses was buried with 'fire rocks' and water wells (*nareh men ihjareh wa-mayteh men ibyareh*). According to Canaan (1927: 88, 110), stones around Nabi Musa are black and contain some bitumen, so they burn when put on a fire. The stones are cut in square or triangular forms, a protective talisman is inscribed, and they are carried as an amulet (*hijab*).

Before the twentieth century, bituminous shale was only rarely used to produce heating fuel, and then usually by Bedouin who chanced to be in the vicinity of such rocks. The extraction of fuel from shale on a regular basis began only during the great fuel shortage of World War I. The Germans produced aviation fuel from bituminous rocks at Makarin, east of el-Hamma, along the Hejaz railway. The Ottomans used petroleum from bituminous shale to fuel locomotives, as well as to power their steam boat on the Dead Sea (Avitsur 1976: 274-77; Bar-Zvi, Abu-Rabia, and Kressel 1998: 50).

The British Mandate in Beersheba terminated in May 1948, as a result of a United Nations Resolution (29 November 1947) to divide Palestine between Jews and Palestinians. Thus, war broke out between Arabs and Jews. Muhammad 'Abd al-Hady was the last Qaimaqam in Beersheba during the British period. The British quit Beersheba on 14 May 1948, in an impressive ceremony attended by Bedouin leaders and senior government officials. The Union Jack was lowered, and the Palestinian flag raised over the Saraya House by the mayor of Beersheba, Mr. Shafiq Mushtaha. Arab rule over Beersheba lasted only a few months, until the capture of the city by the Israel Defence Forces, on 21 October 1948, and the expulsion of its Arabs. Needless to say, as a result of the war no Bedouins stayed in Beersheba (Abu-Khusa 1994: 274-86; al-Dabbagh 1991: 360).

The military cemetery in the western part of Beersheba, near the road to Gaza, is one of the larger cemeteries in the country, containing approximately a tenth of the British Commonwealth World War I dead in Palestine. The British chose Beersheba as the site of the cemetery, because of its scriptural associations and because it was the first city they had captured in Palestine. World War I British Commonwealth cemeteries were in laid out in accordance with guidelines set by the Royal Commission on War Graves, established in 1917. Its basic guiding principle was equality for all soldiers who had died in the Great War. Servicemen of all ranks were to be buried together, in close proximity to where they had fallen, their graves marked by uniform headstones. The cemeteries were to be in the form of an English garden, with lawns, pathways, flowers, and trees. The sanctity of the place was to be indicated by a large stone cross, a Cross of Sacrifice, centrally located, on which there would be a bronze replica of a crusader's sword. The larger cemeteries would also have an altar made of a single stone, the Memorial Stone, containing the words of Psalm 72:17, which has such meaning for Christians: 'May his name endure for ever, his name shall be continued as long as the sun, and men shall be blessed in him, all nations call him blessed'.

The British war cemetery in Beersheba extends, in the form of a square, over an area of two acres, and contains the graves of 1,239 Commonwealth soldiers, arranged in four square burial areas. Opposite the entrance, set in the centre of the wall facing the Gaza road, is a paved openair chapel, behind which a stone cross is prominently set in a high stone wall. At the front of the chapel, a large marble War Stone, which serves as an altar, bears the inscription 'Their Name Liveth for Evermore'. The land of the cemetery was donated by the Beersheba municipality, headed by a Bedouin mayor. The cemetery was built and is maintained by the Commonwealth War Graves Commission. Near the gate, on the wall, is the inscription: 'The land on which this cemetery stands is the free grant of the people of Palestine to whom it was given by the municipality of Beersheba for the perpetual resting place of those of the Allied Armies who fell in the War 1914-1918 and are honoured here'.

The cemetery was dedicated in March 1923 in a solemn ceremony attended by High Commissioner Sir Herbert Samuel and other British government officials and military officers, as well as Bedouin sheikhs and notables. Nearly four-fifths of those buried at the Beersheba cemetery were British, and most of the remainder from Australia and New Zealand. Some fifty of the soldiers were unidentified; their headstones are inscribed: 'A soldier of the Great War known unto God'.

In the centre of the wall to the right is a marble commemorative plaque to eight British and Australian airmen who lost their lives in the skies over the Beersheba region in 1917 and who never found. Their missions involved preventing hostile aircraft from conducting reconnaissance operations or harassing British ground forces. The Ottomans themselves had erected a monument to one of the pilots, in the form of a trapezoidal pyramid, as a chivalric gesture to the prowess of a gallant foe. The British found the stone in January 1918, and made it a memorial to all the fallen British and Australian airmen who died in the area. At the top of the commemorative plaque is the emblem of the Royal Air Force, and underneath is written, 'Sacred to the memory of the names of the fallen airmen', and the dates of their death. At the bottom of the monument is the legend, 'This monument generously erected to one of them by their enemies. Was discovered and restored by their friends. January

1918'. When the cemetery was consecrated, the stone was set in the wall to commemorate the airmen. Their names and the dates of their disappearance were:

1. Capt. F. H. V. Bevan, Gen. List & R.F.C., 19.4.1917
2. 2/Lieut. N. L. Steele, A.F.C., 20.4.1917
3. Lieut. J. S. Brasell, A.F.C., 25.6.1917
4. Capt. C. A. Brooks, Wiltshire Regt. & R.F.C., Attached A.F.C., 8.7.1917
5. Lieut. G. L. Paget, Northumberland Fusiliers, Attached A.F.C., 13.7.1917
6. 2/Lieut. A. H. Searle, A.F.C., 13.7.1917
7. Capt. R. N. Thomas, Gen. List. & R.F.C., 23.7.1917
8. 2/ Lieut. J. W. Howells, Lancashire Fusiliers & R.F.C., 23.7.1917.

Almost all those buried were Christian. One headstone, however, bears a Star of David, marking the grave of Captain S. J. H. van den Bergh, 'Middlesex Yeomanry, 27th October 1917, age 27. Son of Henriette van den Bergh'. He was a London-born Jew of Dutch descent, who was killed to the west of Beersheba five days before the city's capture. He is buried with 79 other British soldiers who died in that action. Captain van den Bergh is buried in the same row as his courageous commander, who was awarded Britain's highest decoration for valour, the Victoria Cross. Captain van den Bergh's parents had inscribed on his headstone: 'So far from home, yet so near to those who love him'.

Behind the military cemetery is a Christian cemetery of just under half an acre. It only came into use in the 1930s (Ettingon 1979: 74; Gal-Pe'er 1991: 103-106). The Muslim cemetery is to north of the city.

Thus are Muslim, Christian, and Jewish war dead buried in ground donated by a Bedouin mayor of Beersheba, symbolizing the coexistence of the three monotheistic faiths in the Holy Land.

Appendix 1

Tribal Court Judges in 1931

According to al-'Aref (1933: 62-69), at the end of 1931 the number of judges was increased from sixteen to twenty, as follows, including the issued dates of the Magisterial warrants:

1. Sheikh Hamd al-Sane', Tarabin, 15.3.1923
2. Sheikh Hsein Abu-Setta, Tarabin, 15.3.1923
3. Sheikh 'Abd-Rabba Abu al-Hssayn, Tarabin, 15.3.1923
4. Sheikh Salman al-Huzaiyil, Tiyaha, 15.3.1923
5. Sheikh Hasan al-'Atawna, Tiyaha, 15.3.1923
6. Sheikh Hsein Abu-Kaff, Tiyaha, 15.3. 1923
7. Sheikh Nasser Abu al-Khayl, 'Azazma, 15.3.1923
8. Sheikh Freih Abu-Meddein, Hanajira, 15.3.1923
9. Sheikh Selim al-Smeiry, Hanajira, 15.3.1923
10. Sheikh Hasan Abu-Jaber, Jubarat, 15.3.1923
11. Sheikh Nemr Abu al-'Udus, Jubarat, 15.3.1923
12. Sheikh Selim Ibn Sa'd, 'Azazma, 30.11.1927
13. Sheikh Salem Abu Samra, 'Azazma 30.11.1927
14. Sheikh 'Iyd Ibn-Rebi'eh, 'Azazma, 30.11.1927
15. Sheikh 'Awda Abu-'Adreh, Tarabin, 30.11.1927
16. Sheikh Mesleh Ibn-Jermy, Tarabin, 30.11.1927
17. Sheikh Salman al-'Urjany, Tarabin, 26.7.1929
18. Sheikh Jaddu' al-'Asam, Tiyaha, 26.7.1929
19. Sheikh Salameh Ibn-Sa'id, 'Azazma, 10.1.1931
20. Sheikh Sallam Ibn-Krayshan, 'Azazma, 10.1.1931

Appendix 2

Palestine Gendarmerie Members in 1933

Al-'Aref (1934:280-281), has left the following partial list of police-men, in 1933:

1. Subhy effendi 'Abd al-Hady, Inspector (*mufattesh*) of the Police Headquarters
2. Hashem effendi al-Dauwdy, Investigation (*tahqiq*) Officer
3. Mr. Levis, a British Officer
4. Mr. Farady, Chief (*ra'is*) of the Police Headquarters
5. Hasan effendi Fares, Inspector (*mufattesh al-kharej*)
6. Ja'far effendi Ahmad Felfel, Secretary Head (*ra'is al-kuttab*)
7. Yusef effendi al-Sarraj, *shawish* No. 467
8. Kamel Felfel, Police No. 416
9. 'Iyd Ibrahim Abu-Irqaiyiq, Police No. 1290
10. Mhammad Yusef al-Dhawahery, Police No. 838
11. Farah Khadder al-Ya'qub, Police No. 1415
12. Mhammad Isma'il al-Ddaher, Police No. 937
13. Fa'yq 'Ayish Abu 'Assy, Police No. 635
14. Hasan 'Abd al-Jabbar 'Abdu, Police No. 311
15. Jawdat Tawfiq al-'Anabtawy, Police No. 255
16. Sliman Dimetry al-Mustakleb, Police No. 971
17. Ragheb Sa'id Abu-Ramadan, Police No. 976
18. 'Abdalla 'Awadd Yunes, Police No. 1329
19. Sharif Sa'id 'Ali, Police No. 1450
20. Karim Rajy Haddad, Police No. 1030
21. Fawzy Iskandar Haddad, Police No. 1449
22. Hanna Khalil Ibrahim, Police No. 1448

23. Nequla Habib Karam, Police No. 977
24. Jeryis Ya'qub al-Ssayigh, Police No. 552
25. Khalil al-Zarad al-Beiby, Police No. 407
26. Sa'id Mhammad 'Assfur, Police No. 316
27. Rajeh 'Abd al-Malek Ibrahim, Police No. 1378
28. Shamrukh Mhammad Hsein, Police No. 234
29. Isma'il 'Ubayd al-Karaky, Police No.1119
30. Sam'an 'Isa al-Hashweh, Police No. 1157
31. 'Awda Mustafa al-Qaryuty, Police No. 1167
32. Mhammad Sa'id 'Abd al-Halim, Police No. 381
33. Mhammad 'Ali Salem, Police No. 438
34. Shukry 'Arafat Mushtaha, Police No. 1132
35. Salman Mhemmed Qabu'a, Police No. 1135
36. Mhammad Abu-Bnayih, Police No. 1315
37. Salman Ahmad al-Gharably, Police No.1292
38. Saleh 'Ali al-Sani', Police No. 1327
39. Salameh Qasem Abu-Hjir, Police No. 1293
40. Salem Abu-Rabi'a, Police No. 1456
41. Salameh 'Awda, attached to police (*buliss idafy*)
42. Musa al-Nmily, attached to police (*buliss idafy*)
43. Saris Hssainy al-'Abid, attached to police (*buliss idafy*)
44. Suweilem Faraj, attached to police (*buliss idafy*)
45. Mhemmed Abu Juwei'ed, attached to police (*buliss idafy*)
    (Al-'Aref 1934: 280-81).

Chapter 4

Education during the British Mandate

After occupying Palestine in 1917, the British divided it into five districts: Jerusalem, Jaffa, Gaza, Hebron, and Beersheba. Upon the establishment of civil government, on 1 July 1920, the number of districts was increased to seven, as follows: Jerusalem, Jaffa, Beersheba, Gaza, Haifa (Phoenicia), Galilee, and Nablus (Samaria). As a rule, municipal councils have remained in office, and with the expiration of their terms, they were replaced by councils nominated by the military governor (Luke and Keith-Roach 1930: 31). From 1920, a dual system of national education was developed, along linguistic and ethnic lines, in Arabic and Hebrew. The Arab system included all schools, both governmental and non-governmental, where Arabic was wholly or mainly the medium of instruction. The system of maintaining schools for Arabic-speaking children in all towns and many villages was continued after 1920 by the government's Department of Education, which was responsible for all government schools in the country in the period under review (the 1920s). The headquarters of the Department were in Jerusalem, and included, in addition to the central clerical and administrative staff, Arab and Jewish inspectorates for the control and supervision of each of the parallel school systems. District inspectorates located in Jerusalem, Jaffa, Nablus, and Acre were responsible for government schools in their areas (Erskine 1935: 198-221; Luke and Keith-Roach 1930: 236-38).

Government Schools

Villages

In 1920, a system was inaugurated whereby Arab villages in which no educational facilities existed were invited to co-operate with the government in establishing elementary schools. The inhabitants of a village would provide a school building and equipment, and if the Department of Education and the Department of Health judged them adequate, the government would appoint and pay for a teacher. The curriculum was comprehensive in nature, covering four years. Many schools had gardens of one to five dunams, where practical instruction in agriculture was given.

Town

Town schools for Arabs increased in both size and number as of 1920, providing a full elementary course of study for boys and girls. Some provided the first two to three years of secondary instruction. In addition, there were training colleges for teachers, technical schools, sports and athletics, agricultural schools for both Arabs and Jews (Luke and Keith-Roach 1930: 238-240; Mar'i 1978: 12-46).

The Government Arab College was originally inaugurated in 1917 to train elementary school teachers. Many graduates went on to do well as students of higher education in Egypt, Syria, the United States, and Great Britain (Erskine 1935: 198-21).

Non-Government Schools

Muslims

The Supreme Muslim Council controlled elementary, secondary, and orphanage schools. The language of instruction was Arabic, although in the higher classes of secondary schools English was also used. There were a large number of *kuttab* schools, where the Quran, reading, and writing were taught.

Christians

Various foreign organisations and religious bodies maintained an interest in education. It should be noted that the majority of non-government schools—Muslim, Christian, and Jewish—received small money grants from the government, based on attendance. All such schools were subject to inspection by the Department of Education, and had to conform to required conditions governing the grants, including regulations related to sanitation (al-Haj 1995: 34-47; Luke and Keith-Roach 1930: 238- 44).

In 1914 the Ottoman authorities estimated the total population of Palestine (Arabs and Jews) at 689,275 (Luke and Keith-Roach 1930: 39). On the establishment of the British civil administration in 1920, the total population numbered some 700,000 (one-tenth Jews). In the 1921/22 school year there were 16,442 Arab students in public schools and 14,239 in private schools (Tibawi 1956: 171, 270). Prior to 1935, only 20 per cent of Muslims children aged 5-15 attended school, compared to 80 per cent among Jews and Christians. In 1945/46, 85 per cent of boys and 65 per cent of girls attended schools in the towns, but in the villages, only 65 per cent of boys and 10 per cent of girls attended schools. In towns children studied six years, and in villages from four to five years (Miller 1985: 98; Palestine Royal Comission 1937: 118). In the 1945/46 school year, the last for which an annual report was published, Arab attendance was as follows: private schools, 43,885 students; and government schools, 81,042 students. Only 64 per cent of children who applied for school admission were accepted. Out of an Arab school-age population aged 5-14, which numbered 300,000 in 1944, only 97,400, or 32.5 per cent, actually attended school, government or private. Out of a Jewish school-age population of 87,000, only 84,000, or nearly 97 per cent, attended school (Tibawi 1956: 66, 167, 171; Government of Palestine II, 1946b: 638). In 1948 when the British mandate was terminated, the official estimate of the Arab population was, in round figures, over 1,300,000; the Jewish population numbered just over 600,000. The growth of the Arab population was due to natural increase, aided by improved health services and material prosperity. The growth of the Jewish population was due to these causes, as well as immigration (Tibawi 1956: 8-9).

The ambition of young, village-born training college graduates working for the Department of Education would almost invariably be to find employment in one of the larger towns; to be sent to a village was viewed as punishment. It was in the towns that they could satisfy their newly acquired expectations of housing and sanitation, and avail themselves of expanded social and cultural opportunities. The Government Arab College, the pinnacle of the selective system of Mandatory secondary education, received approximately two thirds of its students from the villages. Most former villagers were eager to forsake the difficult life they had known for a more promising and convenient one in the towns. Thus, in raising the intellectual, social, and cultural standards of young people, the Arab College and similar institutions also had the effect of estranging young Arabs from their native environment. They tended to drop their native modes of speech and dress, their former preferences in food and drink, and above all, the moral outlook they had been imbued with.

There were exceptions, of course, including some who had gone overseas to study. Such young Arabs stubbornly, and proudly, adhered to the customs and moral code of their people, expressing pride in their place of birth. Yet such as they were few and far between. Only small number of students went abroad, mostly to the United Kingdom, but also to France, Germany, and the United States. Most of those who studied abroad did so at their own expense. However, the Department of Education had also inaugurated a system of selecting a small number of secondary school graduates each year for overseas scholarships, mainly to meet the need for teachers (Tibawi 1956: 67, 245-46).

The socioeconomic structure of Arab society was on the whole semi-feudal. At the top there was a small landed aristocracy, many of whose members were educated and had gained experience in public affairs as officials during the Ottoman regime. Most of the political leaders during the British Mandate belonged to this class. The great majority of the population, however, was composed of the peasantry (*fallahin*), who either owned and cultivated their plots, or served as tenants on the estates of town or country landlords. A small fraction of the urban population engaged in commerce or native industries, but the great majority were labourers.

In addition to the rural and urban populations, there were some 65,000 nomadic Bedouin who lived in the semi-desert area of the Negev, raising cattle and livestock, and engaging in simple agriculture. Though they were a very small minority, their peculiar position received special attention in administrative and educational matters, from both the Ottoman and British administrations. The nomadic Bedouin, who lived in tents and moved camp with the changing seasons, remained little touched by social progress till the last decade of the British Mandate, when, during the period of prosperity, they started to use modern machinery in agriculture, construct stone houses, and demand more school facilities (Abu-Rabiʻa 1994: 7-24; Diqs 1984: 60-87).

During the British Mandate, the prestige of government schools was enhanced by the fact that the lower elementary forms were tuition-free, and tuition for the higher elementary forms and secondary schools was low. Most of those enrolled in government schools were the children of farm labourers, shopkeepers, and artisans. However, the prestige of the government schools was such that even many parents who could afford a private education came to prefer them for their own children. Thus, it was common enough for the son of a common labourer to sit next to the son of his father's employer at school. Furthermore, with moral codes and religious law dominating village life, pupils' dress and manners were much the same, regardless of the social and economic standing of their parents.

Village pupils, as a rule, were undernourished and poorly dressed and shod, yet these circumstances did surprisingly little to hinder their progress. The difficult living conditions of village pupils at town boarding schools induced the headmaster of one such school to open a hostel for boys. The hostel proved so successful that the Department of Education took it over, improving its facilities. However, matters were different in the larger towns, where social stratification and foreign influence resulted in noticeable differences in dress, speech, and diet amongst pupils. Until the early 1930s, the authorities had maintained only one hostel, in Beersheba, for Bedouin pupils, where parents did not have to pay. Beginning in the early 30s, though, several more hostels were opened. They were maintained either privately by school headmasters, or as Department of Education establishments, financed with fees. Government hostels were attached to boys' schools in Tulkarm, Jenin, and Lydda, and semi-official hostels to schools in Hebron, Bireh, Jerusalem, Dura, Majdal, Faluja, Qalqiliya, and Acre. Safad and Nablus provided board and lodging for village boys. The boarding school for Bedouin children at Beersheba accommodated 100 boys (Abu-Rabiʻa 1993: 21-23; al-ʻAref 1934: 272-73; Tibawi 1956: 15; Government of Palestine 1945/46: 7). Exclusively for Bedouin, it was attended almost exclusively by the sons of sheikhs and notables. It was hoped that the school would provide the future tribal leaders with the skills necessary for maintaining relations with government officials (Marx 1967: 34).

The kuttab, whether in a village or town, usually consisted of a single room, in either a private home or public building. A teacher (*khatib*), whose sole qualifications were rudimentary literacy and piety, would instruct some twenty to thirty children, aged 5-12, in the Quran, reading, writing, and arithmetic. Boys and girls would be instructed separately. The children would sit around the teacher in a semicircle or in rows, on the floor in summer and on straw mats in winter. The Quran was usually the only reading material available, and slates and pencils the only writing equipment. The modest fees paid teachers were often tendered in either grain during harvest, or loaves of bread, delivered daily. Though new school equipment and teaching methods had become available, teachers continued to concentrate on the three Rs and religion. Teachers thus proved themselves more accountable to their immediate milieu than to the more removed authority of the Department of Education.

Teachers were looked up to in the villages where they worked, leading fellow Muslims in prayer and serving as village accountant, scribe, and consultant in sundry matters. The communities provided the teacher with free accommodation, with the parents of pupils taking turns serving him meals, and he would be accorded coffee free of charge at the communal guesthouse (*madafeh, diwan*). Sometimes the khatib taught the children under the shade of a tree. For example, in the front of a cave called Magharet Irjal al-Arb'in of Biddu, there is a small grove consisting of two oaks, an olive and a terebinth, whose under shade the khatib taught the children (Canaan 1927: 58).

Among the nomadic Bedouin, a special provision of education was made by appointing peripatetic teachers who lived with the tribes and taught the children in groups (Luke and Keith- Roach 1922: 175). In such cases, the teacher would become intimately linked with the tribe he served. He would live as a permanent guest of the tribe, ordinarily in the guest part of the sheikh's tent (*sheq*), where all his needs were met. Like the village khatib, he would teach the three Rs and Quran in a tent or cave, or under the sky or a tree, where he could give expression to whatever theatrical or demonstrative flair he had. The preferred shade trees to study under were the olive (*zaytun*), Christthorn (*sedreh*), and fig (*teineh*). The teacher's status with the tribe was the same as that of the village teacher with his village. As the tribe moved from one encampment to another, in search of better grazing land and water, the teacher would move with it, his pupils and their parents even doing him the honour of packing his belongings for him.

Over time, the circumstances of the kuttab underwent a complete change. New books, proper desks, and more educated teachers became the norm. So too did permanent school buildings: for the nomadic Bedouin, there was an attractive building, and in the villages, a building atop a hill with modern equipment and books, a workshop, playground, and land for instruction in agriculture. While the scope of such innovation was limited, it was none the less real. The academic subjects taught at school were religion (either Muslim or Christian), Arabic, arithmetic, hygiene, history, and geography. In addition, there were nature studies; instruction in the elements of agriculture, manual training, and practical agriculture; physical training; and drawing. Teaching hygiene was no doubt of great value among the Bedouin tribes. However, an instructor of hygiene could only have aroused incredulity if he was a stickler for keeping to the syllabus and explained the importance of keeping a window open at night, when his pupils slept either in a tent or under the stars.

The system of affording an education to nomadic and semi-nomadic tribes via mobile schools is well-known in the world (Abu-Rabi'a 1993: 21-23; al-'Aref, 1934: 273; Asad 1970: 61-68; Barker 1981: 139-57; Chatty, 1978: 399-415; Cole, 1975:136-63; Gorham, 1978: 1-43; Heron 1983: 61-68; Jabbur 1995: 390-420; Nkinyangi 1981; Shahshahani 1995:145-55; Tibawi 1956: 72-80). According to Musa Saleh Abu-'Ajaj (21 March 1995, personal communication), during the 1940s, Bedouin pupils of the Abu-Rabi'a tribe at the Kuseife school paid the teacher (khatib) a wage of 10 grush and 3 kg each of dried cheese (laban), samen, and eggs. The teachers were: 'Abd al-Hamid from al-Samu'; Dayfalla from 'Azazma; Muhammad al-Massry from al-Samu'. The pupils were: Khalil Salman Abu-Rabi'a, Khalil Sliman Abu-Rabi'a, Mhammad 'Ali Abu- Ma'taq, 'Ali 'Iyd Abu-Rabi'a, Mhammad 'Afnan Qabu'a, Mhammad Faraj al-'Abid, 'Ali 'Ayd al-'Uqayly, Musa Saleh Abu-'Ajaj, Mhammad 'Amer from Drayjat, Shhadeh al-Ghnaymat, 'Abd al-Karim Abu-Ghnaym, Salman Selim al-Krayshy, Ibrahim Abu-'Ajaj, Salman al-Qur'an, Mhammad al-Riyitt, Ibrahim al-Qreinawy, Mhaysen al-Saray'eh, Mbarak Sliman al-Saray'eh, Mhammad 'Iyd al-Saray'eh. The pupils studied up to fourth or fifth grade. Some of them continued in the tribal school at Beersheba, where some of the students were: Salameh Sbayyih Abu-Rabi'a, 'Ali Khalil Abu-

Rabi'a, Mhammad Hasan Abu-Rabi'a, Mhammad 'Iyd al-Saray'eh. It should be noted that 'Ali Khalil Abu-Rabi'a was the Sheikh of the Abu-Rabi'a tribe between 1946-1948.

The question of whether the literacy attained in four years of elementary schooling could be retained under the ordinary conditions of village life intrigued educators. In order to answer it, in 1932 the Department of Education administered standardised achievement tests in language and arithmetic. The test in Arabic set out to assess whether one could read, both aloud and silently, and carry on ordinary correspondence. The test in arithmetic was designed to ascertain proficiency in the four basic operations, as well as multiplication by fractions. Of the 740 persons, with an average of 5.1 years of schooling during the British Mandate, who sat for the tests, 24 per cent failed in Arabic and 18 per cent in arithmetic. These were the results for the country as a whole. In the Negev, which contained some of the country's most advanced and most backward populations, and where the average time in school of those tested was 4.7 years, the failure rate was in Arabic 44 per cent, in arithmetic 23 per cent (Tibawi 1956:219-20).

The British Military administration made three important decisions in the area of education: to supplant Turkish, as the medium of instruction, with Arabic; to open two training colleges with boarding facilities, one each for men and women; and finally, to encourage local education committees that had previously functioned under the Ottoman regime to resume operation. When a village decided to open a school, the British authorities required it to provide a building with adequate facilities, along with an annual sum of 30 STR., which was matched by a state grant in the same amount to pay a teacher's salary of 60 STR. Schools were ordinarily housed in old Turkish buildings, in the courtyards of mosques, or in village guesthouses (*madafa*).

For the twenty years following 1920, the Mandatory administration maintained schools for Bedouin boys in five tribal areas. In the beginning, classes were conducted by peripatetic teachers, who moved with the tribes within the radius determined by arable land, pasture, and water. In time, though, the schools were housed in permanent stone structures located centrally within the tribes' radiuses of movement. In the final decade of the mandatory period the number of tribal schools had risen to over twenty, with half the financial burden borne by the tribes, and half by the British administration.

As in the case of village schools, tribal schools consisted of a single room and a teacher, with the instruction offered at the lower elementary school level; most of those who attended were the sons of the sheikhs and well-to-do tribesmen. From the 1930s, those who had completed the lower forms at tribal schools could attend the upper elementary forms as boarders at the school in Beersheba. In 1932/33, al-'Aref revived the idea of a boarding school for Bedouin. Most of those admitted were sons of either sheikhs or wealthy Bedouin. A literate class of sheikhs and sheikhs' sons had come into being, school graduates who knew how to read and write Arabic and some English. A number of tribal chiefs took the lead amongst the Bedouin tribes and sent their sons to school.

The resulting expansion of the educational system also began to contribute to an integration of tribes: the sons of the various tribes studied together and forged friendships. Bedouin in the Beersheba Qada had their own schools. Some were financed by Bedouin themselves, and some by the British authorities. Schools would be established in one place in a building allocated by several tribes, because in most cases the schools were jointly owned by them. Schools would contain several forms and one or several teachers, depending on the number of pupils.

Particularly noteworthy is the tribal school in Beersheba, which was the central educational institution in the district (Bresslavsky 1946: 251-52). During the British Mandate, the building itself was used as an ordinary, rather than agricultural, school. Boys and girls studied in the same building. Boys entered through the front entrance and studied in the lower-level classrooms, while the girls entered through the back entrance and studied in the upper storey. In 1932/33, when al-'Aref revived the idea of a boarding school for Bedouin, the boys lived in the lower storey and studied in the upper one. The teachers lived either in the building or the neighbouring area. Agriculture made up an important part of the curriculum, and the pupils raised vegetables in the courtyard behind the building. In 1934, the school had a staff of eight teachers and a headmaster. Also in operation as of that year was a girls' school, with three women teachers and a headmistress (al-'Aref 1934: 273). In addition, there were several forms for religious instruction, for Muslims and Christians (Gal-Pe'er 1979a: 296).

Beersheba's importance as the Qada's educational centre becomes all the more clear when one bears in mind that in 1934, there were only five tribal schools in the entire Qada, and they served a school-age population of over 20,000 (Erskine 1935: 198-221). On 30 September 1936, there were 23,400 Bedouin children in the Qada in the 5-15 age group (Government of Palestine 1937a: 153).

Al-'Aref (1934: 272-73) claims that in 1934, over 95 per cent of all Bedouin were illiterate. He does, however, describe them as a people possessing high innate intelligence. The five tribal schools in the Beersheba Qada were: Jarawin, Abu-Setta, Zurei'y, Hanajira, and Jubarat. Each school had one teacher, who taught the children reading and writing, religion, arithmetic, and some history and geography. In Beersheba there were a kindergarten and two schools, one each for boys and girls. The boarders studied, ate, and slept at the facilities at the expense of the British. The boarding-school for Bedouin boys made possible widespread education of Bedouin children who belonged to distant tribes. The idea was well-received amongst the Bedouin, resulting in heavy enrolment and a high achievement level: in the first year, 25 boys enrolled, while in the second, the number went up to 50, and in subsequent years, to 75. Bedouin students had the highest grades in four out of six forms, leaving the peasant, village, and town boys well behind (al-'Aref 1944: 37). The value of education began, if slowly, to dawn on the Bedouin. Al-'Aref once commented that the Bedouin only needed leading. Many former students of that institution have become sheikhs and successful people, amongst them Sheikh Hammad Khalil Abu-Rabi'a, who went on to become a Knesset member (1973-1977, 1979-1981).

Awareness of the importance of education amongst the Bedouin became increasingly strong, particularly in the last decade of the Mandate, with the prosperity engendered by the British military building during the Second World War. As a result of the expansion of educational facilities in tribal areas, Bedouin interested in obtaining an education for their sons tended to wander less, as they had to live within walking, or riding, distance of a school. In the last five years of the British mandate, the Beersheba school had had 90 boarders and 300 day pupils. The boys at the boarding section were encouraged to retain their traditional tribal dress, and were permitted to visit their families' encampments frequently. They had the same academic syllabus, though, as the day pupils, participated in the same sports and extracurricular activities, and were bound by the same discipline. Those amongst them who were selected for secondary studies went on to prove themselves very capable academically.

It was actually the Turks who deserve a good deal of credit for initiating Bedouin education, as they had made serious attempts in the period prior to the First World War to settle, and educate, the Bedouin. They also established a central school in Istanbul for nomad pupils from all parts of the Ottoman Empire (Rogan 1996: 83-107; Me'ir 1997:169-78; Me'ir and Barnea 1985: 18-20; Tibawi 1956: 24-46).

Bresslavsky (1946: 251-52) describes the educational condition of the Negev Bedouin thus: Aside from the regional school in Beersheba and the small elementary school in 'Auja al-Hafir, until 1934 there were only five one-room 'schools' for beginners in Bedouin tents. Still, the proximity of the Bedouin to Beersheba and Gaza, contact with permanent settlements and civilisation, and the economic development of the country in general had nonetheless contributed to furthering their advancement.

In the Negev there arose a very thin crust of young sheikhs and sheikhs' sons who had completed various government schools, including the high school in Jerusalem, although most of them did not complete their studies. During their studies in Jerusalem, in addition to learning some English, they adopted the manners and dress of townsmen, who wore European clothes but continued to wear the traditional headdress (*kufiya/mandil* and *Iqal/marir*). In the 40s, educational activity in the Negev branched outwards, encompassing ever larger groups of people.

Bedouin in the Beersheba Qada had their own schools. Some of them were maintained with funds from the Bedouin themselves, and some with funds from the British authorities. Schools authorised by the director of the Department of Education were considered public schools. Its educational programme was not different from what was common in government school. It imparted to its pupils knowledge of arithmetic, geography, nature study, and agriculture, or rather the science of gardening, which has a central role. The children also took part in sport and games, and had competitions with pupils from cities in the coastal plane, such as Gaza, Majdal, and elsewhere. Their dormitory rooms were large and spacious. Each pupil had a bed and closet for his clothing and personal effects. Dormitory boarders ate in a common dining room, where food was served on trays by pupils on duty. Spoons and forks were also distributed, and the pupils were required to use them as much as possible. Tea was served in porcelain cups. The teachers were urban, in origin and dress. They lived and ate at the school. Sanitary arrangements were adequate.

Shimoni (1947: 146-48) tells us that until 1942 there were only five partial schools with 250 students in the Bedouin tribal area of the Negev. Some of the wealthy sheikhs began to send their sons to other cities, for education, as well as to secondary schools, such as private school in Gaza.

In the final years of the British mandate, when some 300 local boys and 100 Bedouin attended forms 1-7 at the Beersheba school, the building became overcrowded. The girls were transferred to a new building in the neighbourhood, while some of the boys were then transferred to a building on the outskirts of town (Gal-Pe'er 1991a: 89-92).

According to al-Dabbagh (1991: 340-41), Bedouin schools, all of which were for boys, could be divided into two categories: government schools, at which the government paid the teachers' salaries, and tribal schools, whose expenses were covered by members of the tribes.

The table below shows the number of Bedouin schools in the Qada in various years.

Table 4.1   Bedouin Schools in the Beersheba Qada

Date	No. of schools	No. of pupils	No. of teachers
July 1932	8	196	8
July 1938	5	216	5
Jan. 1948	26*	1390**	29***

*   Fifteen of these were tribal schools.
**   Of these, 667 pupils attended tribal schools.
***   Fifteen of the teachers were paid by the tribes.

Source: al-Dabbagh 1991: 340-41.

The tribes, total expenditure on their children's education in 1946/47 was 8,076 guineas. In the late 1940s, there were more applicants to school than there were places for Bedouin children, resulting in many going without an education. In 1947, teachers at Bedouin schools conducted a literacy survey of the tribes. They found that 2,720 Bedouin knew how to read and write, or under 3 per cent of the Bedouin in the Beersheba Qada. Most of the literate Bedouin had merely completed four years of elementary schooling in tribal classrooms; few had completed elementary school, let alone high school. Those who had obtained an education beyond the high school level could be counted on the fingers of one hand (al-Dabbagh 1991: 340-41).

In 1944/45 the Bedouin public school system in Beersheba comprised one boys' school and one girls' school; the seventh form was the highest in both schools (Government of Palestine: Department of Education, 1947: 3-4). In the same scholastic year, in Beersheba's boys' and girls' schools, there were 23 teachers (14 male and 9 female), 715 Muslim pupils (485 boys and 230 girls), and 34 Christian pupils (19 boys and 15 girls), totaling 504 boys and 245 girls. The aggregate expenses of the Beersheba municipality and its inhabitants on the two schools in 1946/47 were 4,306 guineas, of which 3,669 guineas were for new buildings (al-Dabbagh 1991: 359-60).

Muslim schools (non-public) in Beersheba in the 1944/45 school year comprised one private Muslim school (kuttab, apparently), with one male teacher teaching 25 boys (ibid., 20). In Beersheba, the population of children aged 5-15 in October 1944 consisted of 650 boys and 600 girls, of which 504 boys and 245 girls studied in public schools (aside from the kuttab pupils), for a total of 529 boy and 245 girl pupils. Thus, 81 per cent of boys and 41 per cent of girls in the city were in school.

Beersheba: The Boys' School

According to al-Dabbagh (1991:350), the boys' school was basically agricultural, and was intended to prepare young Bedouin to work the land. He further claims (p. 356) that in the Mandatory period, the second storey of the school was used by girls, and the first by boys. This arrangement changed in 1933, when the Department of Education decided to open a boarding school for boys; the second floor was then used as a dormitory, and the first for classrooms, while the girls moved to a rented building. The boys' school was situated on a twenty dunam plot of land, seven dunams of which were allotted to a garden, for agricultural instruction. There was also a carpentry shop. In addition, the Department of Education built six new rooms to accommodate the additional pupils who applied each year. The structure, which had been intended to accommodate twenty-five Bedouin youngsters as boarders, had to accommodate a hundred in 1946/47. The school had a library, which had 1,455 volumes as of 1 July 1947 (al-Dabbagh 1991: 356-58; Encyc. Palest. 3: 59-60).

The table below indicates the rate of progress in education during the British period and the fierce desire of the Bedouin to obtain an education. The data are for boys alone.

Table 4.2 Rate of Progress in Bedouin Education during the British Period

Year	No. of classes	No. of pupils	No. of teachers and headmaster
1919/20	4	180	5
1920/21	5	184	6
1933/34	8	266	8
1947/48	14	580	17

Source: (al-'Aref 1934: 282-83; al-Dabbagh 1991: 340-58).

The breakdown of the 580 boy pupils in 1947/48 by form is as follows:

> First form (2 classes) 115
> Second form (1 class) 53
> Third form (2 classes) 85
> Fourth form (2 classes) 107
> Fifth form (2 classes) 89
> Sixth form (2 classes) 65
> Seventh form (2 classes) 43
> Eighth form, the first year there had been a pre-high school form, (1 class): 23 pupils (Source: (al-'Aref 1934: 282-83; al-Dabbagh 1991: 340-58).

Al-'Aref (1934: 282-83), mentions that in the year 1933, some of the staff were:

1. Mahmud affendi al-Safariny (headmaster)
2. 'Abd al-Latif affendi 'Abidyn (teacher)
3. al-Sheikh Selim affendi 'Awwad (teacher)
4. Anwar affendi al-Khatib (teacher)

5. Sulayman affendi al-Huseiny (teacher)
6. Antun affendi al-Turk (teacher)
7. 'Abd al-Khaleq affendi Yaghmur (teacher)

It should be noted that Mr. Abd-Alla Ibrahim al-Khatib was the headmaster of the boys' school in Beersheba from 1939 to 1948 (al-'Aref 1973).

Beersheba: The Girls' School

Until 1933 girls studied on the second floor of the boys' school. In that year, as has been mentioned, the second storey was converted to a boys' dormitory. The girls' school was moved to a rented building. In 1946/47, construction of a school building for girls commenced on a 13-dunam plot of land. In the summer of 1947, three rooms were completed at a cost of 3,269 guineas, with the government contributing 1,500 guineas and the remainder being paid by the Beersheba municipality. In 1948, construction commenced on an additional four rooms, with the government contributing another 1,500 guineas, and the remainder of the necessary funding coming from the Beersheba municipality.

One should bear in mind that this school had been in existence since the beginning of the British conquest of Beersheba, consisting of one classroom and one woman teacher. In the 1931/32 school year, the girls' school had an enrolment of 158 pupils, who were instructed by four women teachers, in forms one through four. In 1942/43, the school completed the entire elementary school span of forms one through seven.

On 1st July 1947, the school had a library with 651 volumes (al-Dabbagh 1991: 358-59).

As of 1 January 1948, the girls' school had eight women teachers and a headmistress, with an enrollment of 300 pupils, distributed by form as follows:

First form (2 classes) 110
Second form (1 class) 52
Third form (1 class) 51
Fourth form (1 class) 41
Fifth form (1 class) 26

Sixth form (1 class) 12
Seventh form (1 class) 8 (al-Dabbagh, 1991: 358-59).

Beersheba: Kindergarten

A kindergarten began to function on 22 July 1946, in a rented building. It was established by a special committee. As of 1 January 1948, it had 90 pupils, 23 of whom were girls. The pupils' parents paid tuition. Two nursemaids taught at the kindergarten. In 1945/46, the income of the kindergarten committee was 2,381 guineas; against 637 guineas were paid in expenses.

The Mandatory End

The British Mandate over Palestine terminated in May 1948, as a result of the United Nations Resolution (27 November 1947) to divide Palestine between Jews and Palestinians. A bloody war broke out between Arabs and Jews. The Egyptian Army took over the buildings of the boarding school when it captured the city in May 1948. When the Israeli Defence Forces captured Beersheba on 21 October 1948, it was in this building that Commander Mahmoud Riad of the Egyptian Army and Israeli Chief of Operations Yiga'el Yadin negotiated a ceasefire. The school building was taken over by the Israeli Southern Command. In June 1949, the first floor of the building was turned into a soldier's recreation centre, and the second into living quarters (Abu-Khusa 1994: 274-86; al-Dabbagh 1991: 360; Gal-Pe'er 1979a: 269-98; 1991b: 89-92).

Bedouin Tribal Schools

A complete list of tribal schools in the Bedouin public school system in 1944/45, according to Government of Palestine's: Department of Education 1947: 3-4), appears below. The number in parentheses to the right of the school name indicates the highest form in the school. Additional data about tribe and clan are given in brackets.

Tribal Schools

> Abu-Jaber (4) [Abu-Jabir tribe, Jubarat Clan]
> Abu-Ghaliun (4) [Abu-Ghalyun, Tarabin Clan]
> Abul Haj (3) [Abu al-Hajj, Tiyaha Clan]
> Abu-Mulliq (4) [Abu-Mu'eileq, Tarabin Clan]
> Abu-Sitta (4) [Abu-Setta, Tarabin Clan]
> Abu-Yahya (3) [Abu-Yehya, Tarabin Clan]
> 'Ara'ra (3) ['Ar'ara/'Ar'ere, Dhullam Clan]
> Al Baha (4) [al-Baha, Tiyaha Clan]
> Hanajra (4) [Hanajirat Abu-Meddein, Hanajira Clan]
> Huzayyil (2) [al-Huzaiyil, Tiyaha Clan]
> 'Imara (3) [al-'Imara, Tarabin Clan]
> Jabarat (4) [May be Deqs School, Jubarat Clan]
> Jammama (2) [al-Jammama, Tiyaha Clan]
> Khalasa (3) [al-Khalasa, 'Azazma Clan]
> Khizali (3) [Khez'aly, 'Azazma Clan]
> Khwailfa (4) [Khuweilifa, Tiyaha Clan]
> Kusaifa (4) [Kuseife, Dhullam Clan]
> Nusairat (2) [Nuseirat, Hanajira Clan]
> Shu'th (3) [al-Shu'uth, Tarabin Clan]
> Zurei'i (4) [al-Zurei'y, Tarabin Clan]

It should be noted that though there are statistical discrepancies between my sources, I have decided to rely on them, because they are official documents.

Bedouin Schools by Clans

The data below relate to 1 January 1948, unless otherwise stated.

Hanajira

The number of literate persons in the Hanajira clan in 1947 has been estimated at 500, out of a total population of 7,125 (al-Dabbagh 1991: 406-12). They were served by two schools:

1. Hanajira School, also called Hanajirat Abu-Meddein School, was founded in 1924 and was located twelve kilometres south of Gaza. The pupils numbered 75, and

were divided into four forms taught by a single teacher. The
school was built near the tomb of Sheikh Nabhan, over
which a mosque was built. Pilgrims light candles there;
likewise, believers swear by, and on, the sheikh (Bar-Zvi,
Abu-Rabi'a, and Kressel 1998: 101).

2. Nuseirat School was situated on a site known as al-
   Demaytha (Dathen), about five kilometres east of Deir al-
   Balah. Founded in 1944, the school was attended by 69
   pupils in three forms, taught by one teacher.

Jubarat

In 1947, the estimated number of literate persons in the Jubarat clan
was 200 out of a total of 7,528 clan members (al-Dabbagh,
1991:413-416). The clan had two schools maintained by the government, and one maintained by the tribe.

1. Deqs School founded in 1925, was located seven kilometres
   east of Bureir. It had 55 pupils in four forms, which were
   instructed by one teacher.
2. Abu-Jaber School, founded in 1944, was located forty two
   kilometres north west of Beersheba, ten kilometres from al-
   Faluja. The site, known as Bir Abu-Jaber, is 170 metres
   above sea level. The school had 58 pupils in four forms,
   instructed by one teacher.
3. Thawabteh School was approximately four kilometres
   south of Bureir and five kilometres west of Abu-Jaber
   School. The school, which opened on 1 August 1945, had
   43 pupils in four forms instructed by one teacher, who was
   paid by the tribe.

Tarabin

The Tarabin clan is one of the largest, and wealthiest clans (in land).
In 1931, its estimated population was 16,284. By the summer of
1947 it had reached 32,381, of whom an estimated 1,200 were literate (al-Dabbagh 1991: 420-28). The clan had eight schools, five of
them maintained by the government and three by the clan's tribes.

TARABIN GOVERNMENT SCHOOLS

1. Abu-Setta al-Ma'in School, founded in 1924, had 75 pupils
   in five forms. They were instructed by two teachers, both

paid by the government. It was located eight kilometres
east of Bani Suheila.

2. al-Shuʿuth School, founded in 1945, had 51 pupils in four
forms, instructed by one teacher. It was located some ten
kilometres north of Khuzaʿa in the al-Shuʿuth
concentration known as Quz al-Shaʿth.

3. Abu-Muʿeileq School, founded in 1940, had 45 pupils in
four forms instructed by one teacher. It was located eleven
kilometres south of Gaza near the Palestinian Sulphur
Quarries.

4. al-Zureiʿy School, founded in 1925, had 73 pupils in four
forms, instructed by two teachers, one paid by the
government and the other by the tribe. It was located eight
kilometres from Abu-Setta School and seven from Hanajira
School.

5. Abu-Ghalyun School, founded in 1927, had 125 pupils in
five forms, instructed by two teachers paid by the
government. It was located twenty kilometres west of
Beersheba.

Tarabin Tribal Schools

1. Abu al-Hussain School, founded in 1947, had 56 pupils in
three forms, instructed by one teacher paid by the tribe. It
was located seven kilometres east of Abu-Setta School, at a
site known as Kuz Suleiyib.

2. Abu-Yehya School, founded in 1944, had 54 pupils in four
forms, instructed by one teacher paid by the tribe. It was
located eight kilometres west of Beersheba on a hill known
as al-Breij.

3. Al-ʿImara School, founded in 1945, had 67 pupils in four
forms, instructed by one teacher paid by the tribe. It was
located twenty nine kilometres west of Beersheba on lands
owned by al-Ghawaly.

Tiyaha

The population of the Tiyaha clan was estimated at 13,708 in 1931.
By the summer of 1946 it had reached 25,153 (including the Dhullam), of whom some 600 were literate in 1947 (al-Dabbagh 1991:
344-434). The clan had nine schools, two of which were maintained
by the government.

TIYAHA GOVERNMENT SCHOOLS:

1. Abu al-Hajj School, which opened on 1 January 1945, had 61 pupils in four forms, instructed by one teacher paid by the government. It was located twenty five kilometres north-west of Beersheba, at Ghazala.
2. Al-Huzaiyil School was located twenty five kilometres north of Beersheba, at a site known as Zubala. Zubala in Arabic means 'little water'. The school closed in 1933 because of low enrolment and irregular attendance by those enrolled, but it re-opened in 1944. It had 36 pupils in four forms, instructed by one teacher paid by the government.

TIYAHA TRIBAL SCHOOLS

1. Shlaliyin School, which opened in 1947, had 45 pupils in two forms, instructed by one teacher paid by the tribe. It was located about six kilometres north of al-Huzaiyil School, at a site known as al-Mantra, south-east of Tall al-Mleiha (al-Malha).
2. Al-Baha School, which opened in 1941, had 55 pupils in four forms, instructed by one teacher paid by the tribe. It was located seventeen kilometres south-east of Gaza, about four kilometres from the Gaza-Beersheba road.
3. Qudeirat School, founded in 1946, had 53 pupils divided into four forms instructed by one teacher who was paid by the tribe. It was located at Umm Betin, some seventeen kilometres north-east of Beersheba.
4. Al-Jammama School, was opened on the site of a former government school which had been forced to close in 1933, because of irregular attendance. The school that later existed was founded in 1944. It had 42 pupils in four forms, instructed by one teacher at tribal expense. It was located thirty nine kilometres north-west of Beersheba, twenty five kilometres north-east of Gaza, seven kilometres from Jubarat School, and about fourteen kilometres from al-Huzaiyil School.
5. Khuweilifa School, founded in 1941, had 59 pupils in four forms, instructed by one teacher paid by the tribe. It was located twenty four kilometres north-east of Beersheba and about ten kilometres west of the Beersheba-Hebron road.

Dhullam

There were some literates, educated by kuttabs, but no one knows how much.

1. Kuseife School had 39 pupils in four forms, instructed by one teacher paid by the tribe. It was located some thirty kilometres east of Beersheba, at Kharbet Kuseife (al-Dabbagh 1991: 442).
2. 'Ar'ara School was founded in 1944, when instruction was conducted in an old cave. In 1946 the school moved to a new building, which was built by the tribe at a cost of 450 guineas. The school had eighteen pupils divided into four forms, instructed by one teacher paid by the tribe. It was located twenty nine kilometres south-east of Beersheba, at Kharbet 'Ar'ere (al-Dabbagh 1991: 442-43).

'Azazma

In 1931, the population of this branch is believed to have been 8,678. By the summer of 1946, it had approximately doubled, reaching 16,370. In 1947 the estimated number of literate persons in 'Azazma clan was 220 (al-Dabbagh 1991: 455-59; Abu-Khusa 1979: 26-27; Kirk 1941: 60). There were four schools, all of which were maintained by the tribe.

1. Al-Khalasa School was established by the government after the British conquest, but closed because of irregular attendance. It reopened in 1941, with fifty three pupils in four forms, instructed by one teacher retained at the tribe's expense. The school was located fifteen kilometres north-west of 'Asluj.
2. 'Auja School had also been established by the government, but was closed in 1932 because of insufficient enrolment and irregular attendance. It was reopened at tribal expense in 1945. It had twenty three pupils in three forms, instructed by one teacher at tribal expense. The school was located seventy four kilometres south-west of Beersheba.
3. 'Asluj School, established by the tribe in 1946, had 36 pupils in four forms, instructed by one teacher paid by the tribe. The school was located thirty one kilometres from Beersheba, on the Beersheba-'Auja road.

4. Khez'aly School, founded in 1943, had twenty four pupils in four forms, instructed by two teachers paid by the tribe. It was located fourteen kilometres south of Beersheba on a site known as Buq'at al-Khez'aly, whence came the name of the school.

Sa'idiyin

The Sa'idiyin clan had an estimated aggregate population of 645 in 1931. Neither al-'Aref nor al-Dabbagh mention anything about the clan having schools. Al-Dabbagh notes that there was no one in the clan who knew how to read or write (al-Dabbagh 1991: 470-73).

Aheiwat

In 1931 the Aheiwat clan's estimated population was approximately 420, and in 1946, some 1,000 (IDF 1954: 14; Marx 1967: 11). No mention is made of them having a school (al-Dabbagh 1991: 474-76).

Appendix 1

Beersheba's Governors: *Qaimaqam*s

The Beersheba Governors during the British Mandate, according to al-'Aref (1934: 262-63) were: Capt. B. B. Ragless, Major Chatwin, A. Nathan, Kenny Leveck/Levik; Robert Edward Crosbie (PIF 446); Cartright; Morris Bailey (PIF 78); Champion, Sir Reginald Stuart (PIF, 421); Abdel-Razzaq effendi Kleibo [Qlibu], 'Aref al-'Aref. According to Abu-Khusa (1994: 278), Mr. Muhammad Abd al-Hady was the last Qaimaqam in Beersheba.

'Aref al-'Aref (1892-1973) was perhaps the most noteworthy of these figures. A writer and public figure who saw himself as an Arab nationalist, he was born in Jerusalem, where he attended elementary school. He went on to Istanbul for his secondary education, and then studied political science at university there. Upon completion of his studies, he worked as a translator in the Ottoman foreign service. In the First World War, he served as a junior officer in the Ottoman army on the Caucasus front, and was taken prisoner by the Russians. After years of captivity—two of them in Siberia—he escaped.

At the end of the war, he returned to Mandatory Palestine and founded the newspaper *Suria al-Jenubia*, 'South Syria', which reflected a pan-Arab viewpoint. An anti-Zionist, he was sentenced by the British authorities to ten years' imprisonment for having a hand in the incitement that led to the eruption of violence in Jerusalem in April 1920. He escaped to Syria, where he was active in the 'Syrian Congress'.

After the fall of the Faysal regime, he found refuge in Trans-Jordan. British High Commissioner Herbert Samuel granted him a pardon, and he returned to western Palestine. He took up employment with the mandatory government, serving as Qaimaqam in Jenin,

Nablus, Beisan, and Jaffa. From 1926 to 1928, he was loaned to the Trans-Jordan government, where he served as First Secretary. In the period from 1929 to 1939, he was Qaimaqam of the Beersheba Qada, and from 1939 to 1942, was Qaimaqam of Gaza. In 1943 to 1948, he was Qaimaqam of Ramallah. After annexation of the West Bank to Jordan, he served as Mayor of Jerusalem (1950) and a minister in the Jordanian government (1955). 'Aref al-'Aref published books on the history and laws of the Negev Bedouin, and histories of Jerusalem and Gaza (PEI 1983: 369; Aurel and Cornfeld 1946: 51-52).

Appendix 2

High Commissioners of Palestine: *Mandub Samy*

1. *Samuel, Herbert Louis,* first Viscount Samuel (1870-1963). Liberal politician, administrator, and philosopher. His great grandfather immigrated to Britain from Poland. Samuel learnt Hebrew as a child and also was raised in strict conformity with Jewish beliefs and customs. He was proud to be a Jew. He was educated at London University College, then at Balliol College, Oxford, where he gained a first class degree in history. Samuel had a long association with the Liberal Party. In 1902, he was elected to Parliament. In 1905 he was appointed Under-Secretary of State at the Home Office, rapidly making a name for himself in the field of social legislation. In 1908, he took the oath of Privy Counceller, and in 1909 he joined the Cabinet as Chancellor of the Duchy of Lancaster.

As early as 1914 he talked about the possibility of settling Jewish refugees in Palestine, and from time to time during the First World War Samuel placed memoranda before the Cabinet advocating Jewish claims. In 1917 the Balfour Declaration stated that the British Government viewed with favour the establishment in Palestine of a national home for the Jews, without prejudice to the civil and religious rights of existing non-Jewish communities in Palestine. In 1914 Samuel became president of the Local Government Board. From January to December 1916 he served as Home Secretary, but spent the remainder of the First World War on the back benches. In 1920, when Britain was granted a mandate to administer the country, Samuel became the first High Commissioner of Palestine. Before accepting the post in July 1920, he sought assurance that his Jewish sympathies would not be considered a hindrance to his impartiality as an administrator. Upon receiving his appointment, he was knighted. During his service in Palestine, Samuel identified himself as Jewish, occasionally attending religious services. Asquith wrote about Herbert that 'he is a Jew of the Jews'. When Samuel's term of office ended in 1925, he and his wife planned to settle as private citizens in Palestine, but this was unacceptable to the Government and Samuels decided to live in Italy, eventually returning to London (D.N.B. 1961-1970: 918-22; P.E.I., 1983: 361).

2. *Plumer, Herbert Charles Onslow,* Field Marshal, the First Viscount Plumer of Messines (1857-1932). Educated at Eton, Plumer was an adjutant at age twenty-two, and in 1882 he was promoted to captain. In 1890 he was appointed deputy-assistant-adjutant-general at Jersey, a position which entailed training as well as administrative responsibilities. Plumer fought against the Boers in South Africa, and commanded troops on the Western Front in 1917. In August 1925 Plumer accepted the office of High Commissioner of Palestine, to which Trans-Jordan was added in 1928. With his stern personality, both Jewish settlers and Arabs realised that while he would sympathetically listen to them, he would allow no disorder. The work was strenuous, especially when carried out with his thoroughness, and the toll taken by the war contributed to the strain. He resigned in July 1928. In 1929 he was ennobled with a viscountcy (D.N.B. 1931-1940: 702-706; P.E.I. 1799-1948: 400).

3. *Chancellor, Sir John Robert* (1870-1952), soldier and administrator. He was educated at Blair Lodge, Polmont, and the Royal Military Academy, Woolwich, being commissioned in the Royal Engineers in 1890. After a period of service in India, he attended the Staff College and in 1904 was appointed assistant military secretary to the Committee of Imperial Defence.

In 1906 he was made secretary of the Colonial Defence Committee. In the period from 1911 to 1916, he served as governor of Mauritius, and from 1916 to 1921 he served as governor of Trinidad and Tobago. In 1918, he was promoted to lieutenant-colonel. From 1923 to 1928, he was the first governor of South Rhodesia, after which he was High Commissioner for Palestine and Trans-Jordan until 1931. After disturbances at the Wailing Wall in Jerusalem in 1929, which involved violent Arab attacks on the Jews, the Government issued a statement on policy in October 1930 which went to what Chancellor undoubtedly regarded as the root of the Palestine problem. When in 1931 a white paper was in effect reinterpreted by Ramsay MacDonald in a statement to Chaim Weizmann, Chancellor's faith in government policy in Palestine was badly shaken. His disappointment was reflected in his speech at a farewell banquet in Jerusalem, when he said: 'I came hoping to increase the country's prosperity and happiness. I am leaving with my ambition unfulfilled. Conditions were against me.'(D.N.B. 1951-1960: 206-207; P.E.I. 1799-1948: 421).

4. *Wauchope, Sir Arthur Grenfell* (1874-1947), soldier and administrator. Educated at Repton, in 1893 he was commissioned into the Renfrew militia battalion of the Argyll and Sutherland Highlanders. He fought in the Boer war, and in Mesopotamia at Kut and Baghdad. He spent the whole of the First World War commanding troops on the line, except when in hospital with wounds. In 1923 he was promoted to major-general, under which rank he held four appointments: military member of the overseas settlement delegation to Australia and New Zealand (1923), chief of the British section of the Inter-Allied Military Commission of Control in Berlin (1924-27), general officer commanding the 44th Home Counties Division (1927-29), and command in Northern Ireland (1929-31).

In 1931 Wauchope was appointed High Commissioner and Commander-in-Chief for Palestine and High Commissioner of Trans-Jordan. Wauchope embarked upon his task with application and devotion. He was a man of high ideals, cultivated tastes, tireless energy, and a considerable personal fortune. Hospitable and generous with his own resources, many projects and institutions, Jewish and Arab, owed much to his purse and to his eager interest in agriculture, public health education, Arab villages, and Jewish colonies. He encouraged both the native arts of the indigenous Arabs and the imported European cultures of the Jews. He encouraged ventures such as the Palestine Symphony Orchestra and the town planning of Jerusalem. He acted vigorously during the Arab insurrection of 1936-38, but although the excesses of the Arabs were curbed, the troubles continued. Wauchope's health was already frail, and the troubles took their toll; he relinquished office in February 1938.

The only portrait known to exist is a crayon drawing by an unknown Palestinian artist in the possession of the Black Watch (D.N.B. 1941-1950: 930-932; P.E.I. 1799-1948: 185).

5. *MacMichael, Sir Harold Alfred* (1882-1969), a colonial civil servant. In 1901 he won the public school fencing championship. In the same year he also won an open scholarship to Magdalene College, Cambridge, where he obtained first class honours in the first part of the classical tripos in 1904. In 1905 he took a first class in the Arabic examination for the Sudan Political Service.

In 1905 he began work in Khartoum, Sudan, and was then sent to Kordofan. In 1912, he published a book on the pedigrees and customs of the tribes of northern and central Kordofan, and in 1913 he published a monograph on the various camels of Kordofan. At the end of 1918, while on leave in England, he escorted a delegation of Sudanese notables who came to London to congratulate the King on his victory. He held several additional posts overseas. In 1933, he became the governor of the mandated territory of Tanganyika, and in March 1938, he was appointed High Commissioner and Commander-in-Chief for Palestine and High Commissioner for Trans-Jordan. MacMichael came to Palestine as a man blessed with good Arabic, writing, reading, and speaking, but no Hebrew at all. The Jews, therefore, saw him as biased and hostile. Only when his papers were opened at the British Public Record Office did the Jews realise how justly he had judged them. It should be noted that both Jew and Arab found him stern but resolute in unpleasant duties, including mobilisation of all manpower and property, dictation of the crops to be grown, and for the Jews, deduction of the number of immigrants who had arrived illegally from their quota of immigration certificates.

With the liberation of Africa and the removal of the German threat to Palestine, Jewish terrorism increased, and on 8 August 1944, the Stern Gang made a determined attempt to murder MacMichael and his wife. MacMichael was unhurt, but Lady MacMichael was slightly wounded; MacMichael's aide-de-camp and driver were both seriously wounded. But MacMichael's term of office was up, anyway, and he left Palestine in September 1944 (D.N.B. 1961-1970: 704-706; P.E.I. 1799-1948: 324-25).

6. *Vereker, John Standish Surtees Prendergast,* First Viscount Gort (1886-1946). He was educated at Harrow, and went on to the Royal Military College, Sandhurst. He was gazetted an ensign in Grenadier Guards in 1905. In 1914 he was promoted to captain and went to France. He attained note when on 27 September 1918,

while in the successful offensive against the passage of the Hinden-
burg line near the village of Flesquieres, he found himself tem-
porarily in command of the 3rd Guards brigade. He was severely
wounded but continued to direct the attack and was awarded the
Victoria Cross.

Gort attended the Staff College on its reopening in 1919. In
1921, he was promoted to lieutenant-colonel and returned to the
Staff College as an instructor. In 1926 he became chief instructor at
the Senior Officers' School at Sheerness, and rose to colonel. He
went on to command the Grenadier Guards and a regimental district
in 1930, became director of military training in India in 1932, and in
1936 took command of the Staff College, Camberley. In 1937 he
was appointed military secretary to the secretary of state for war,
and later in the year, Chief of the Imperial General Staff, skipping the
intermediate rank of lieutenant-general to become full general. In
1941 he went to Gibraltar as governor and commander-in-chief. The
outstanding accomplishment of his service in the war of 1939-45
was his organization of the defence of Malta from 1942 to 1944, an
achievement rewarded by promotion to field-marshal in 1943.

On 31 October 1944 Gort was appointed High Commissioner
and Commander-in-Chief for Palestine and High Commissioner for
Trans-Jordan. He ardently looked forward to taking up his responsibilities there. However, a serious illness compelled him to resign
on 21 November 1945, and he died in London on 31 March 1946.
It was during this last illness in 1945 that the viscountcy in the peer-
age of the United Kingdom was conferred upon him. During his
tenure in Palestine, he tried to improve relations between the Government, Arabs, and Jews (D.N.B. 1941-1950: 904 -907; P.E.I.
1799-1948: 127).

7.   Cunningham, Sir Alan Gordon, (1887-1983). In November
1945, Cunningham was appointed High Commissioner and Commander-in-Chief for Palestine and High Commissioner for Trans-
Jordan. He was to be the last British High Commissioner for
Palestine. After the adoption on 29 November 1947, of the UN resolution to partition Palestine between Jews and Arabs, Cunningham
and the British administration had difficulty in imposing their
authority on the country. When Cunningham set sail from Haifa
harbour on 14 May 1948, the British Mandate over Palestine came
to an end (Aurel and Cornfeld 1945; P.E.I. 1799-1948: 441).

Chapter 5

Negev Bedouin Education
1948–1998

Estimates of the Bedouin population in the Negev at the end of the British Mandate vary from 65,000 to 103,000 (Shimoni 1947: 3-46; IDF, 1954: 1-22; Marx 1967: 2-34; Abu-Khusa 1979:7-75; Muhsam 1966). The Negev Bedouin were divided into ninety-five tribes, which were part of great tribal clans (confederations): Tarabin, Tiyaha, Dhullam, Jubarat, Hanajira, 'Azazma, Ja halin, Sa'idiyeen and Aheiwat (al-'Aref 1934: 6-87; Marx 1967: 2-34). When the Israeli Army conquered the Negev in October 1948, the majority of the tribes were expelled to Jordan, the Gaza Strip, and the Sinai (Diqs 1967:5-63; Higgins 1969: 147-149; Marx and Sela 1980). Other Bedouin who had participated in hostilities against Israel left the Negev because they were afraid of the Israeli authorities (Abu-Khusa 1994: 7-75; Abu-Rabi'a 1994b: 7-9). The situation remained unstable until 1953, when only about 11,000 Bedouin were left in the Negev (Abu-Rabi'a, 1994: 8; Marx 1967: 12).

Most of the Bedouin who remained were remnants of tribes or belonged to small tribal branches; they banded together around nineteen tribal heads recognised by the Israeli authorities as sheikhs. These groupings were concentrated under military rule in the north-eastern Negev, in a closed area. Anyone wanting to enter or leave the area had to obtain a special permit from the military authorities and at times even movement within the region, between one tribe and another, required a permit. Sheikhs and notables were given special permits which allowed them freedom of movement out of the closed area, on condition that they returned to their tribe by evening. Military government was repealed in 1966.

Development of Education: 1948-1998

According to the Israeli Ministry of Education (1951: 348-349), the following were listed for schools the Bedouin tribes in the 1950/51 school year:

Table 5.1   Bedouin Tribal Schools, 1950/51

Tribal school	Teachers	Classes	Boys	Girls	Total pupils
Abu-Rabi'a	1	2	42	—	42
Abu-Ghalyun	1	5	33	—	33
Al-'Asam	1	3	35	—	35
Abu-Qreinat	1	2	35	—	35
al-Huzaiyil	2	4	47	—	47
Abu-Irqaiyiq	2	4	36	—	36
al-Talalqeh	1	2	43	—	43
al-'Azazma	1	2	58	—	58
al-'Uqby	1	3	31	-	31
Total:	11	27	360	—	360

These schools, according to the author, were listed before the expulsion of certain tribes.

Source: Israeli Ministry of Education 1951: 348-49.

Bedouin Pioneers in Education

According to Musa Saleh Abu-'Ajaj and Dr. Yunes Ibrahim Abu-Rabi'a (21 March 1995, personal communication), in the 1952/53 school year, four Bedouin pupils were sent to Terra Santa College (boarding school) in Nazareth to continue their studies. The following year, an other group of seven pupils, followed them. The eleven pupils were:

1. Mhammad Salman Abu-Rabi'a
2. 'Iyd 'Awda Abu-Rabi'a
3. Musa Saleh Abu-'Ajaj
4. Sliman Saleh Abu-Ajaj (Pupils numbered three and four were brothers).

5. Yunes Ibrahim Abu-Rabi'a
6. Yusef Ibrahim Abu-Rabi'a (Pupils numbered five and six were brothers). Pupils numbered from one to six were from the Abu-Rabi'a tribe).
7. Mhammad 'Ali Abu-Qreinat
8. Salman 'Ali Abu-Qreinat (Pupils numbered seven and eight were brothers from the Abu-Qreinat tribe).
9. Yusef Khalil Abu-Siyam,
10. Mhammad 'Arad al-Qreinawy
11. Salem Salameh al-Huzaiyil (Pupils numbered nine to eleven were from the al-Huzaiyil tribe).

Each pupil paid about 40 *dinar*s a month in fees and tuition to the college.

During the 1956 war between Israel and Egypt, their parents brought them back to their tribes for several months, then sent them back to the college. In subsequent years, some of the sons of sheikhs and notables continued their studies at Nazareth. In 1959, the first pupils of the group graduated: Musa Saleh Abu-'Ajaj and his brother Sliman Saleh Abu-'Ajaj.

The author has succeeded in collecting a number of biographical details through interviews with members of these two groups, who were the pioneers in education and held posts among the Negev Bedouin society, they also were a good sample to be imitated.

Mhammad Salman Abu-Rabi'a left the school in the eleventh grade for personal reasons. His sons were educated at Israeli universities; three of them became teachers and one of them, Salem, the principal of Kuseife junior high school. Mhammad was one of the leaders of the Abu-Rabi'a tribe, before his tragic death in a road accident in 1970.

'Iyd 'Awda Abu-Rabi'a left the school in the eleventh grade to get married. He sent his sons to Israeli universities. Three of them became teachers and one of them, 'Ali, is a teacher and well-known journalist.

Musa Saleh Abu-'Ajaj and his brother Sliman Saleh Abu-'Ajaj were appointed the first two Bedouin teachers in the Negev, in the new State of Israel. Later on, both of them became the first Bedouin principals of Bedouin schools. Musa, at first appointed to a position at Kuseife school, was the teacher and principal of the school where the present author studied.

Sliman Saleh Abu-'Ajaj, at first appointed to a position at Abu-Irqaiyiq tribal school, moved to Hura, Tel-Arad, and Kuseife.

Yunes Ibrahim Abu-Rabi'a graduated in 1962. He continued his academic studies at Hadassah Medical School at the Hebrew University of Jerusalem and graduated in 1970, as the first Bedouin physician (M.D.) in Israel. He then worked in the Ministry of Health and at Soroka Hospital, Beersheba. Later he became the Director of the Bedouin Rahat Medical Centre, and a specialist in diabetes at the Soroka outpatient clinics. He is married and the father of four girls and one boy. Two of his girls are students at Ben-Gurion University of the Negev. His wife, Jihan Abd al-Qader, from a Nazareth family (her family was originally from Lubia), became a supervisor of a Bedouin kindergarten under the Ministry of Education, in the Negev.

Yusef Ibrahim Abu-Rabi'a, the brother of Yunes, left the College in tenth grade, studied electrical work, and became a self-employed electrician. His children are educated; one of them (Salem) is a teacher.

Mhammad 'Ali Abu-Qreinat left the school for personal reasons. He later became a sheikh, succeeding his father after his death.

Salman 'Ali Abu-Qreinat, the brother of pupil 7 the above, left the school for personal reasons. After his brother's death in 1997, he succeeded him as sheikh.

Yusef Khalil Abu-Siyam became manager of a building company.

Mhammad 'Arad al-Qreinawy became a manager of Leumi Bank.

Salem Salameh al-Huzaiyil travelled to the United States, studied psychology and education, obtained a master's degree, and became a businessman.

These first two groups of graduates were the Bedouin pioneers of secondary education. Their friends, who could financially afford it, followed them.

Continuing Expansion

According to Marx (1967: 13, 44-45), the Bedouin population in the Negev in 1960 was 16,000. Until 1960, most Bedouin schools —eight out of nine—were built near the encampments of tribal sheikhs, thus giving children of their tribes a higher than average chance to acquire literacy. Sheikhs headed the tribal education committees established to raise funds for the construction of school buildings, and thus could influence decisions on siting. In the 1960/61 school year, only seven of the schools were open: Abu-Irqaiyiq, Abu-Rabi'a, al-Huzaiyil, al-

Asad, al-'Atawna, and Mas'udiyn al-'Azazma. There were 556 registered pupils, out of an estimated 4,000 children of school age, meaning that only some 14 per cent of Bedouin children attended school. Some of the tribes' peasant (*fallahin*) children attended, and paid for, private classes conducted by a young tribesman. State elementary schooling was free. In 1960/61 there were only two Bedouin teachers, the other Arab teachers being non-Bedouin from northern Israel. The two teachers were brothers: Sliman and Musa Saleh Abu-'Ajaj, from the Abu-Rabi'a tribe, mentioned above.

According to Gavron (1965: 24-28), in 1965, when there were some 20,000 Bedouin in the Negev, 1,100 Bedouin pupils attended fourteen schools, 68 per cent of which offered only three lowest forms. Only three of the fourteen were complete primary schools. Some of the older children from outlying encampments would live by themselves in tents around the school; they looked after themselves admirably in these improvised boarding schools. In that school year, there were thirty-five Arab teachers from northern Israel teaching in the Negev. There were also five Bedouin teachers, two of whom have became principals of Bedouin schools.

According to Bernstein-Tarrow (1978: 141-47), in the 1976/77 school year there were 6,552 Bedouin pupils in twenty two schools, staffed by 249 teachers. Fourteen of these schools were headed by Bedouin principals. According to Abd al-Kadir (1978: 94-95), in 1978 there were 300 teachers, both men and women, 220 of whom were Arabs from northern Israel. In September 1975, a training class at Kaye Teachers College in Beersheba opened to prepare Bedouin teachers.

In 1998, there were approximately 106,000 Bedouin in the Negev. About 61 per cent of them lived in seven permanent towns planned by the Israeli authorities. The seven towns and their populations are: Rahat, 30,000; Tel-Sheva [Tel al-Saba'], 8,000; Kuseife [Ksifa], 5,000; 'Aro'er ['Ar'ara], 7,000; Segev Shalom [Shgib al-Salam], 4,000; Hura, 7,500; and Laqiya, 3,500). The other 45,000 Bedouin lived according to traditional tribal patterns: huts of wood, metal, or baked mud; tents made of goat hair, jute bags, or plastic sheets; houses built of blocks of stone. In the tribal areas there are primary schools and health services. Primary and secondary schools are situated in each one of the seven towns, as are clinics. Beersheba has Soroka Hospital and outpatient clinics, which are open seven days a week, twenty four hours a day.

Table 5.2   Bedouin Pupils and Total Bedouin Population in the
Negev, 1950-1998

Year	Pupils	Boys (%)	Girls (%)	Bedouin population
1950/51	360	100%	—	12,740
1953	No official or estimated details			11,000
1960/61	556	100%	—	16,000
1965	1,100	91%	9%	20,000
1970	2,659	84%	16%	30,000
1975	5,306	77%	23%	40,000
1980	10,356	67%	33%	50,000
1985	15,222	61%	39%	60,000
1990	20,704	59%	41%	75,000
1995/96	29,966	55%	45%	95,000
1997/98	35,124	54%	46%	106,000

Source: Abu-Rabi'a 1997; Abu-Rabi'a, Aref, and Dov Barnea 1998.

The 1997/98 School Year

By the 1997/98 school year, there were 35,124 Bedouin pupils from kindergarten to twelfth grade, studying in fifty one schools, eight of which were secondary schools, and the others primary and junior high schools. There were 1,700 teachers, men and women, in this educational system. About 60 per cent of them were Negev Bedouin. The other 40 per cent were Arabs from the Galilee (*al-Jalil*) in northern Israel, and the so-called Little Triangle (*al-Muthallath*). There were 320 Bedouin students and teachers in training at Kaye Teachers College of Beersheba, and about 150 Bedouin students at Ben-Gurion University and other universities in Israel.

Table 5.3   Distribution of Bedouin Pupils in Grades 1, 8, and 12, 1997/98

Grade	Total pupils	Boys (%)	Girls (%)
1	3,817	52 %	48%
8	2,303	56%	44%
12	1,075	61%	39%

Source: Abu-Rabi'a, Aref, and Dov Barnea 1998.

Bedouin Pupils' Progress

In 1984/85 there were 2,048 pupils (1,088 boys and 960 girls) in the first grade. When they graduated from twelfth grade in 1995/96, only 911 pupils remained (579 boys and 332 girls). The dropout rate among Bedouin pupils was thus 56 per cent, with 47 per cent of boys and 65 per cent of girls quitting of schools (Abu-Rabi'a 1997; Abu-Rabi'a and Barnea 1998.). For more details on Bedouin dropout rates see Abu-Saad 1991,1998.

It should be noted that Bedouin students have graduated as follows from Ben-Gurion University:

1975-79: 2 male students
1980-84: 3 male students
1985-89: 26 male students, 1 female student
1990-94: 35 male students, 5 female students
1995-99: 62 male students, 10 female students

Source: The Center for Bedouin Studies and Development, Ben-Gurion University of the Negev, 1999.

Dropping out of School:
Reasons and Solutions to the Problem

Motives for Discontinuing Education

Leaving school early—dropping out—is a critical problem among the Bedouin which requires a solution based on the recognition of its various contributing factors and causes. Many factors of various kinds are liable to cause, or encourage, quitting school in Bedouin society. Most of them are of a social, cultural, or economic nature, the most important being large families; polygamy (the author has the impression that over 15 per cent of Bedouin men are married concurrently to two, three, or even four women); marital problems among parents; parental neglect; the social status of the family; the need to help with the household and help support the family; a limited degree of interest on the part of parents, particularly older parents, in the education of their children; and early betrothal (which usually results in immediate withdrawal from school, especially of girls). Other factors are poor grades, health problems, lack of motivation, and various social or economic pressures.

Some families that own businesses, such as construction companies, or sheep or camel breeding establishments, encourage their children to begin working in the family business at an early age. Such parents do not see quitting school as an educational catastrophe, but rather as a welcome addition to the family workforce and income. Furthermore, the epidemic of drug abuse has begun to make itself felt in the Bedouin community, leading young pupils to leave school early.

Factors related to tradition and religion also cause youngsters to leave school at an early age. Some families take their daughters out of school at the end of eighth, or even sixth grade, to help their mothers at home. Also, to this day, there are families that withdraw their daughters from school upon the onset of puberty, for fear of any violation of the honour of the family. In such families, the children usually marry at the end of seventh or eighth grade, and in the course of the ninth, some of the boys become fathers. The schooling of virtually all Bedouin girls who become engaged to marry is immediately discontinued by their families.

Sometimes schools themselves are the cause of early discontinuation of studies. Most schools fail to take adequate steps to prevent early leaving, and at times even encourage it, especially among poor or troubled youngsters. The author has the impression that teachers and class tutors generally do not adhere to the guidelines contained in a circular on school leaving early issued by the Ministry of Education.

Parents, too, play a attitudes are most influenced. Some parents do not visit their children's schools or attend PTA meetings, do not take an interest in their children's progress and sometimes do not even know what grade their children are in. A number of reasons account for the lack of involvement of such parents, among them apathy towards formal education and a view of the family's livelihood as their primary concern. This state of affairs may lead their children to feel they are free of parental supervision, leading in turn to a decline in scholastic achievement.

VIOLENCE IN THE SCHOOLS

Such parents usually take an interest in their sons at school only when they are involved in violence, as either attackers or victims. Bedouin parents' sensitivity to the matter of violence is so great because of its possible connection to intra-tribal or inter-tribal violence, even murder. Therefore, parents and heads of extended families, and tribal elders, often intervene decisively to put an immediate end to school violence.

In this context, it is worth remembering that the school is a meeting place of many youngsters from all the tribes in an area. Any dispute, quarrel, or altercation (to say nothing of murder), involving the tribes is reflected at school, and vice versa. Bedouin pupils at a school are not just individuals, but also members, and representatives, of families and clans; it is possible to gauge any friction within a tribe or town by the level of friction at school. The author wishes to emphasise that there is no difference in this respect between a tribal school and a school in a Bedouin township. Sometimes, in fact, familial and tribal relationships are even more keenly felt in township schools than in schools in the periphery, because of their crowded conditions and proximity to residential neighbourhoods.

Thus, being at school confers no immunity from violence, and oft-times pupils constitute convenient targets for the settling of familial or tribal scores. It should be borne in mind that three out of seven comprehensive secondary schools were established in the wake of tribal murders, rather than out of pedagogical considerations. Hundreds of pupils, and scores of teachers and headmasters, have been transferred from their original schools to schools in other settlements so as to avoid proximity to a hostile population. Reality on the ground has dictated to the Ministry of Education patterns of activity appropriate to dealing with problems of different sorts.

There are times when pupils who perform poorly in their studies, or are physically weak or too young to look after themselves in difficult situations, find themselves ejected from the school system at an early age. School authorities, who are often anxious to rid themselves of such pupils, are often involved in a conspiracy of silence.

Violence of all kinds is prevalent in Bedouin society, in schools as much as elsewhere. The violence applied by some teachers to pupils can result in the pupils themselves becoming violent: towards teachers, other pupils, society as a whole, towards the school and school property, even towards their parents. At times, a pupil struck by a teacher or headmaster complains to the police; a pupil usually takes such a step with the encouragement of his classmates or parents, or third parties who have a score to settle with the attacker. In such cases, family heads, teachers, and headmasters usually make a concerted effort to calm matters down, before they are brought to the attention of the police or Ministry of Education. There have been cases of parents or pupils going back to the police within a few days of lodging a complaint, accompanied by representatives of community dignitaries, to cancel the complaint. The withdrawal of a complaint is sometimes an explicit condition in agreements of reconciliation between opposing tribes or extended families.

Under conditions such as those discussed here, it is Bedouin tradition that invariably prevails when there is a conflict between tribal tradition and Israeli law. Arrest, interrogation by the police, trial, and prison do not absolve an attacker from Bedouin justice.

CULTURAL AND SOCIOECONOMIC FACTORS

Some of the findings of the present study indicate that there are differences in the dropout rates among different strata of a given school class, as well as between boys and girls; the findings have also indicated that enforcement of the Compulsory Education Law has been partial. The findings indicate that dropping out increases from the seventh grade, and is particularly pronounced amongst girls. The reasons are usually social and cultural, and sometimes economic. They derive from Bedouin tradition and attitudes concerning the proper place for girls at that age, aside from anxiety lest the honour of the family be violated. As the income of families declines, or its dependence on traditional sources such as raising livestock increases, the more likely their children are to leave school early. Parents have been known to discontinue their children's studies because they could not afford such expenses as new school clothes and shoes, textbooks and copybooks, pencils and pens. Some children of poorer families attend school without necessary textbooks and copybooks, and are equipped with only one pen and perhaps two pencils for an entire school year. The burden of helping economically disadvantaged children is borne by the teachers and pupils from more affluent homes; disadvantaged children receive virtually no assistance from the local authorities or Ministry of Education.

It is amongst such children as these that quitting school is most prevalent. Poverty induces some children to work to help support their families; also, difficult economic circumstances tend to sharpen the urge to attain economic independence at an early age. The scholastic attainments and self-image of such youngsters are generally lower than those of classmates with higher scholastic achievement. To this is added the factor of teachers' preconceptions about pupils who perform poorly, which in turn reinforce their low self-esteem. Such feelings of inferiority often result in youngsters leaving school early, especially amongst the lower socio-economic strata. Needless to say, there are teachers who judge their pupils by such external factors as scholastic attainment, their dress, accent, skin colour, and family or tribal status; such teachers thus make a negative contribution to bridging the gap between social strata.

It is worth noting in this context that in the 1995/96 school year, there were all of four truant officers in the Bedouin sector—four full-time positions for a school population of 29,966, from kindergarten to twelfth grade.

Recommendations

In brief, the main causes of quitting school amongst the Bedouin are social, cultural, economic, and religious-traditional. The necessity of migrating with livestock, and perhaps other factors, may also contribute to the phenomenon. The matter of young Bedouins quitting school must be dealt with in a thorough, systematic, and consistent manner, under the supervision of an official of the Ministry of Education who is assigned to the Bedouin sector on a full-time basis. Such an official would be responsible for supervising all matters related to dropping out, and would be in direct contact with truant officers in the Bedouin townships, temporary settlements, and tribal concentrations. Mayors, town councillors, the municipal management of Rahat, public figures, sheikhs and other Bedouin dignitaries, headmasters, and class tutors must all assume a role in helping to deal with the problem of school dropouts. They must not allow handling of the matter to devolve on government ministries, even the Ministry of Education; they must under no circumstances be permitted to lay the blame elsewhere. They must give full support to those working in the field. Laying the blame on parents or the Ministry of Education misses the point, and harms rather than helps the effort to deal effectively with the problem. The time has come to work rather than blame, and the sooner the better.

A unit should be established to prevent children from quitting school and help young Bedouin in the townships get on their feet in life. Such a unit should be staffed by people from a variety of disciplines and walks of life: people skilled in supervisory work, truant officers, social workers, community representatives, clergymen, sheikhs and dignitaries. It should also have at its disposal well-trained field workers in all the disciplines that touch upon the problem, as well as a nurse, a doctor, and a psychologist, whenever the need arises. This team of professionals would have to deal with family problems, and even problems arising between neighbours and tribes, when they threaten to cause young people to leave school; the team would work closely with family members. In other words, a unit must be established that is entirely dedicated to dealing with the problem of school dropouts amongst the Negev Bedouin.

The proposed unit would have a mandate to perform the following tasks:

- Ascertainment of compliance with the Compulsory Education Law in Bedouin schools and assessment of what is being done at those schools to deal with the problem of dropouts. It would be incumbent upon every headmaster to personally handle, along with class tutors, the problem of quitting school at his school. The headmaster would report weekly on every case of dropping out to the appropriate authorities in his township and the Ministry of Education. Statistics related to quitting school dropouts would be published for each township at the end of each month, trimester, and school year. These statistics would be reported to the district inspector by the education ministry official responsible for superrising the problem of dropouts.
- Development of ancillary and alternative institutions, such as youth employment programmes in the Bedouin sector.
- The expenditure of any effort to prevent dropping out. Once a pupil leaves school, it is very difficult, if at all possible, to bring him back, because of his personal feelings and the possibility of rejection by his classmates, and even by his teachers. Teachers tend to assume that a serious youngster simply does not quit school.
- Allocation of resources, both human and budgetary, to schools and local authorities which have experienced the problem of school dropouts of any kind.
- The hiring of competent educational counsellors for Bedouin schools.
- The establishment of an inter-ministerial committee, perhaps involving the Ministry of Education and the prime minister's office, that would be charged with working to

improve economic conditions in the Bedouin sector, enhancing its environmental development, and dealing with the neighbourhood problems that exist under a backdrop of social tensions. Likewise, special attention must be paid to Bedouin who live outside permanent settlements; their cardinal problems must be seriously addressed.

- The organisation of public forums in communities, to increase the awareness of parents and the community at large. In the light of the findings of the present study, the author would also recommend.
- Rewarding schools that significantly reduce the incidence of quitting.
- Improving the appearance of school entrances and the overall school environment;
- developing an educational facility for desert agriculture, which would include, among other projects, the cultivation of medicinal herbs;
- developing a secondary school system solely for girls, as an additional option to existing facilities;
- developing private schools, in addition to existing facilities;
- furnishing the school population with health services;
- providing pupils with hot meals at school.

A Concluding Word about School Early Leaving:

The author believes that caution should be exercised in drawing conclusions about the Negev Bedouin on the basis of conditions in Western countries, including Israel. Even when considering a single group, caution should be exercised in drawing analogies from one period to another. The Negev Bedouin are in a state of transition from a traditional to a Western society. Such a transition may be likened to a whirlpool: it is abrupt, complex, and sometimes slow; the beginning of wisdom is often to approach it with caution, so that it does not spin out of control, finally leading to tragedy. There must be no clash with Bedouin parents in the matter of 'authority' over their children, either in what relates to school, or in general. The approach embraced must be cautious, and based on persuasion, reasoned argument, and friendliness; such an approach has proved effective time and again over the years. The processes of socialisation, modernisation, and integration are related to that of cultural adaptation. Education is but one component among many. It behooves one to remember that Bedouin tradition, spanning as it has several millennia, cannot be superseded in a single modern generation.

I only regret not having been able to bring to school Swilem and Swilmeh, the proverbial Bedouin boy and girl who did not enjoy the blessings of an education. It but remains for me to say to them, 'Rejoice in the path you have chosen, perhaps it has been your lot.'

In the name of Allah, the Beneficent, the Merciful: "Naught of disaster befalleth in the earth or in yourselves but it is in a Book before We bring it into being—Lo! That is easy for Allah. That ye grieve not for the sake of that which hath escaped you, nor yet exult because of that which hath been given. Allah loveth not all prideful boasters" (Quran 57:22-23).

Appendix 1

List of Schools and Names of Principals
(1997/98 school year)

K = Compulsory Kindergarten; PK = Pre-Kindergarten; Cl.= Class;
Special Ed.= Special Education; B = Boy; G = Girl

School ID#:	Name	Principal name	Grades	Cl.	B	G	Total
Rahat							
618058:	al-Huzaiyil	Sultan al-Huzaiyil	K, 1-8	20	309	298	607
618249:	al-Salam	Nawwaf al-Qreinawy	PK, K, 1-6	27	494	477	971
618264:	al-Zahra	Samir al-Huzaiyil.	K,1-6	33	583	572	1,155
618298:	Bayt al-Hekma.	Sabry Hmeid.	K,1-6	28	517	421	938
618231:	Ibn-Khaldun	Ibrahim al-Huzaiyil	K,1-8	20	351	314	665
618322:	'Umar b.al-Kattab	Khalil al-Qreinawy	K,1-6	26	476	394	870
618348:	al-Aakha	Diab al-Afinesh	K,1-6	20	357	320	677
618371:	Salah al-Din	Salem al-Qreinawy	K,1-6	16	241	245	486
618363:	Abu-'Ubayda	Hasan al-Nasasteh	K,1-6	10	161	153	314
618447:	Ibn-Sina	Sliman al-'Abid	K,1-6	8	101	117	218
627000:	Special Ed.	Mrs.Majdulina Hammud	1,2,4,7-9	9	54	17	71
648048:	Comprehensive *Shamela*	'Ali al-Qreinawy	7-12	34	702	538	1,240
648113:	al-Nur '*Idadyia*	Salem al-Qreinawy	7-9	21	434	362	796
648030:	Secondary	Sliman al-Huzaiyil	9-12	24	463	327	790
Pre-Kindergarten			PK	13	249	241	490
Total:			PK+K,1-12	309	5,492	4,796	10,288
'Amal Technical		Mhammad al-Qutnany	10-12	13	257	10	267
Total in Rahat:			PK+K,1-12	322	5,749	4,806	10,555

K = Compulsory Kindergarten; PK = Pre-Kindergarten; Cl.= Class;
Special Ed.= Special Education; B = Boy; G = Girl

School ID#:	Name	Principal name	Grades	Cl.	B	G	Total
Tel-Sheva							
618223:	Abu-Bakr-A	ʻAbd-Rabba al-Mekkawy	1-6	18	273	301	574
618413:	Abu-Bakr-B	Salameh Abu-Ghanem	K,1-6	18	297	250	547
618140:	Jubran Khalil	ʻAttiya Abu-Taha	K,1-6	21	359	332	691
618421:	al-Resalah	Mhammad Abu-Riyash	K,1-4	10	164	165	329
678011:	*ʻIdadyia*	Yusef Abu-Saʼd	7-9	21	353	361	714
800144:	ʻAmal Secondary	Musa Abu-Ghanem	10-12	19	243	211	454
Pre-Kindergarten			PK	8	124	121	245
Total in Tel-Sheva:			PK+K,1-12	115	1,813	1,741	3,554
Kuseife:							
618041:	Hammad Abu-Rabiʻa	Musa Abu-Rabiʻa	K,1-6	22	382	341	723
618132:	Tel al-Melh	Mhammad al-ʻUmur	K,1-8	29	443	471	914
618173:	Tel Kasif	Sliman Saleh Abu-ʻAjaj	1-8	26	429	406	835
627018:	Special Ed.	Ismail Abu-ʻAjaj	1-9	13	48	41	89
800037:	*ʻIdadyia*	Salem Abu-Rabiʻa	7-9	12	251	188	439
800144:	ʻAmal Secondary	Nayif Abu-Rabiʻa	10-12	19	477	195	672
Total in Kuseife:			K,1-12	121	2,030	1,642	3,672

K = Compulsory Kindergarten; PK = Pre-Kindergarten; Cl.= Class;
Special Ed.= Special Education; B = Boy; G = Girl

School ID#:	Name	Principal name	Grades	Cl.	B	G	Total
ʻArʻara							
618280:	Abu-ʻArar	ʻAttwa al-Qerm	K,1-6	31	504	521	1,025
618314:	Ibn-Sina	Ibrahim al-Sarayʻeh	K,1-6	23	425	331	756
648071:	Comprehensive/ Shamela	Sliman al-Zabarqa	7-12	32	601	430	1,031
Total in ʻArʻara:			K,1-12	86	1,530	1,282	2,812
Shgib al-Salam							
618330:	Shgib al-Salam-A	Ibrahim al-Jarabʻeh	K,1-6	25	474	405	879
618405:	Shgib al-Salam-B	ʻAbdalla al-Jerjawy	K,1-6	24	374	392	766
648071:	Comprehensive	Mhammad al-Hamamdeh	7-12	31	658	388	1,046
Pre-Kindergarten:			PK	1	5	4	9
Total in Shgib al-Salam			PK,K, 1-12	81	1,511	1,189	2,700

School ID#:	Name	Principal name	Grades	Cl.	B	G	Total
Laqiya							
618082:	Laqiya-A	Mhammad Abu-'Ayish	K,1-6	27	417	444	861
618397:	Laqiya-B	Musa al-Sane'	K,1-6	20	356	371	727
648055:	*'Idadyia*	Yusef al-Asad	7-9	15	262	254	516
648097:	Secondary	Khalil Abu-'Ayish	10-12	12	183	201	384
Total in Laqiya			K,1-12	74	1,218	1,270	2,488

K = Compulsory Kindergarten; PK = Pre-Kindergarten; Cl.= Class; Special Ed.= Special Education; B = Boy; G = Girl

School ID#:	Name	Principal name	Grades	Cl.	B	G	Total
Hura							
618074:	Hura	Talal al-'Atawna	K,1-6	29	530	478	1,008
618066:	al-'Atawna	Faruq al-'Atawna	K,1-8	19	279	271	550
644203:	Comprehensive	Sa'id al-Nebbary	7-12	23	379	327	706
Total in Hura			K,1-12	71	1,188	1,076	2,264
al-'Azzeh							
618215:	al-'Azzeh	Mhammad al-'Azzeh	K,1-8	3	16	17	33
Tribal Schools: (Sultat al-Ma'aref al-Badawiya):							
618108:	al-'Azazma	Sultan Abu-M'ammar	K,1-8	25	500	392	892
618090:	al-Sayid	Salman al-Qreinawy	K,1-9	27	497	405	902
618462:	al-Amal	Khalil al-Khurm	K,1-6	9	129	119	248
618165:	al-'Asam-A	Mhammad Abu-Sbit	K,1-9	26	431	386	817
618355:	al-'Asam-B	Ismail al-'Asam	K,1-9	23	393	324	717
618017:	Abu-Kaff	'Ali Abu-Kaff	K,1-8	18	299	272	571
618181.	al-Turshan	Musa al-'Atawna	K,1-9	26	459	386	845
618207:	al-Fur'a.	Salem Imtirat	K,1-8	16	312	214	526
618033:	Abu-Qreinat	Yusef Abu-'Ayadeh	K,1-8	15	269	210	479
618116:	Tel-Arad	Adib Abu-Rabi'a	K,1-8	9	116	111	227
618199:	al-Hawashleh	'Isa al-Hawashleh	K,1-9	22	303	330	633
618454:	Kuhla	'Ali Abu-Rabi'a	K,1-6	9	99	90	189
Total in Tribal Schools				225	3,807	3,239	7,046

Negev Clans and Tribes
Sheikhs and Notables

Tarabin

*A*ccording to Israeli estimates, the Tarabin numbered about 21,000 in 1931 (IDF 1954: 15; Marx 1967: 11). Other resources put their population in 1931 at approximately 16,284 (8,814 males, 7,470 females), and in 1948, approximately 32,000 (al-Dabbagh 1991: 420; Abu-Sitta 1994). According to Bailey (1981: 46), in 1981 there were approximately 21,500 Tarabins in the Gaza strip.

Below is an enumeration of the Tarabin tribes and their sheikhs, during and after the British Mandate.

Najamat al-Sane'

Hamd Hamdan al-Sane' from Najamat al-Sane' of Tarabin was born into the Najamat al-Sane' tribe in the late nineteenth century. He attended primary school within his tribe, then continued in Beersheba School. He was subsequently sent to study in Istanbul.

One of the prominent leaders of his Najamat al-Sane' tribe in the Tarabin clan, he became the sheikh of his tribe around 1920. He was made a member at the Tribal Court (*Mahkamat al-'Ashair*) in Beersheba on 15 March 1923. As early as 1932, Sheikh Hamd al-Sane' and Sheikh Ibrahim al-Sane' were mentioned as representatives of the "Arab Committee of Palestine" in the city of Beersheba. After the 1948 war between Israel and Arabs, part of the tribe, including Sheikh Hamd, was forced to move to Jordan, where Sheikh Hamd was appointed to the Jordan Senate (*Majles al-A'yan*). After his death he was succeeded by his son, Sheikh Hammad, who was eventually succeeded by his brother, Sheikh Dayfalla Hamd al-Sane', the current sheikh, who earlier served as an officer in the army (*Ra'id*). Several families were expelled in 1948 to the Gaza Strip. Other families, some 156 souls, stayed in the Negev under Sheikh Sliman 'Iyd al-Sane' (Abu-Khusa 1994: 137-38; al-'Aref 1933: 44, 68; 1934: 79-81; Bar-Zvi 1977: 1-13; Gal-Pe'er 1979a: 284; IDF 1954: 15, 28).

Najamat al-Sufy

Ahmad Mhammad al-Sufy was appointed sheikh in 1930 (al-'Aref 1933: 44; 1934: 79-81). After the 1948 war, Sheikh Ahmad al-Sufy, with most of his tribe, was expelled to the Gaza strip (IDF 1954: 15). Upon his death, he was succeeded by Sheikh Hmeid Mhammad al-Sufy; other families were expelled to Jordan under Sheikh Hammad 'Ayyad al-Sufy (Abu-Khusa 1994: 142). According to Bailey (1981: 47), as of 1981 al-Sufy were distributed in the Gaza Strip as follows: Rafah region, 300; Rafah refugee camp, 1,135; Khan Yunis refugee camp, 905; Deir al-Balah region, 540.

Najamat Abu-'Adra

'Awda Selmi Abu-'Adra was appointed sheikh in 1920 (al-'Aref 1933: 44; 1934: 79-81). After the 1948 war, Sheikh Salman 'Awda Abu-'Adra, with most of his tribe, was expelled to the Gaza Strip (IDF 1954:15). According to Bailey (1981: 47), the Abu-'Adra refugee population in the Gaza Strip in 1981 was as follows: Khan Yunis region,100; Khan Yunis refugee camp, 390; Deir al-Balah refugee camp, 120; Rafah refugee camp, 300.

Other members of the tribe mainly Shuyukh al-'Iyd, were expelled to Jordan, while a few families stayed in the Negev (Abu-Khusa 1994: 139).

Najamat Abu-Sussein

Mhammad Mansur Abu-Sussein was appointed sheikh in 1920, (al-'Aref 1933: 44; 1934: 79-81). After the 1948 war, Sheikh al-Hajj Mhammad Abu-Sussein was expelled to the Gaza Strip (Abu-Khusa 1994: 139; IDF 1954: 15). According to Bailey (1981: 47), there were 360 Abu-Sussein tribesmen living in the Rafah refugee camp in 1981.

Najamat al-Qesar

Salman Selim al-'Urjany was the sheikh of the Najamat al-Qesar tribe in 1930s (al-'Aref 1933: 44; 1934: 79-81). After the 1948 war, Sheikh Mesleh Ibn-Jarmy, with most of the tribe, was expelled to the Gaza Strip. Some of the tribe stayed in the Negev, with the al-Sane' tribe (Abu-Khusa 1994: 140; IDF 1954: 15). According to Bailey (1981: 47), in 1981 there were 1,500 al-Qesar living in the Rafah region, 228 in the Khan Yunis region, 320 in the Deir al-Balah refugee camp, 1,200 in the Rafah refugee camp, and 1,218 at the Khan Yunis refugee camp.

Najamat Abu-Suhayban

Mhammad 'Ibyd Abu-Suhayban was the sheikh of the Najamat Abu-Suhayban tribe in the 1930s (al-'Aref 1933: 44; 1934: 79-81). He attended primary school at his tribe's school, then continued at the Beersheba School. He was one of the sons of the tribal elite sent to study in Istanbul; later he became sheikh of the reunited Dawabheh and N'aymat tribes, of Tarabin. After the 1948 war the Sheikh Abu-Suhayban of the Dawabheh tribe was forced to move to the Gaza Strip, while some families stayed in the Negev. (The N'aymat tribe, with Sheikh Dhaysh al-Qady, was expelled to the Gaza Strip. IDF 1954: 15).

According to Bailey (1981:47), the distribution of the Abu-Suhayban in the Gaza Strip in 1981 was as follows: Rafah refugee camp, 1,164; Khan Yunis refugee camp, 445.

Ghawaly Abu-Sitta

During the British Mandate, tribal leader Sheikh Hsein Dahshan Abu-Sitta served as a member of the Tribal Court and Agricultural Council (al-'Aref 1933: 44; 1934: 82-89). In 1935, he became one of the founders of the Palestinian Arab Party, and in 1941, he was a member of a delegation of Palestinian Arabs to the High Commissioner. Towards the end of World War II, he resumed an active rule in the affairs of the Palestine Arab Party, becoming a member of its Executive Committee. In the 1948 war, he collaborated with Muslim Brotherhood volunteers who entered the country. In May 1948, the Israel Defence Forces blew up his home, because he and members of his tribe had taken part in hostile activities against Jewish settlements.

After the 1948 war, Sheikh Hsein and his tribe were expelled to the Gaza Strip. In September 1948, he became a member of the

Palestinian National Council in Gaza (Abu-Khusa 1994: 129-130; IDF 1954: 15; Shavit et al. 1983: 13).

According to Salman Abu-Sitta (1995: 18), and the Ma'in Abu Sitta Society (1994), Sheikh Hsein Dahshan Abu-Sitta, a tribal statesman and pioneer of Bedouin education, became a sheikh in 1918. He traveled to Egypt many times. He was impressed by the reformist movement led by Sheikh Muhammad 'Abdu, and by the Arab National Revolt.

Born in 1882, he learnt to read and write in a *kuttab* school, and became well cultivated by reading and mixing with learned men. He built the first tribal school in 1920 at his own expense, and contributed to second school in 1946. He brought in a succession of teachers: Abdullah al-Khudary (the first), Tawfik al-Halimy, Salman al-Massry, and Muhammad Abu-Liyya (the last).

In 1921, together with other Palestinian dignitaries, Sheikh Hsein met Churchill at the Government House in Jerusalem. He represented Southern Palestine in the Palestine Agricultural Council in 1929. In addition, he attended the Fifth Arab Palestine Congress (1922), the Sixth (1923), the Seventh (1928), the National Committees Congress in Jaffa (1936), and the Arab National Congress at Bludan in Syria (1937). He was a signatory to the All-Palestine Government on 1 October 1948. He was also a member of the Arab Higher Committee and the Higher Islamic Council in Gaza.

Sheikh Hsein was keenly interested in education. He sent his sons and nephew, Abdalla, to schools in Jerusalem, and encouraged others to do the same. After the Mandatory government refused to grant his sons scholarships to study in England, he sent them to Egyptian universities. By 1948, almost all his sons had graduated; they included a lawyer, a doctor, and several engineers.

Sheikh Hsein died in exile in Gaza, in 1970.

According to Bailey (1981: 48), in 1981 the Ghawaly Abu-Sitta were distributed in the Gaza Strip as follows: Deir al-Balah refugee camp, 130; Khan Yunis region, 120; Khan Yunis refugee camp,180; Rafah refugee camp,180; and Rafah region, 400.

Sheikh Abdalla Musa Abu-Sitta

One of the most important leaders of the Tarabin tribes, Abdalla Musa Abu-Sitta was born in 1914 and grew up under the care of his uncle, Sheikh Hsein Abu-Sitta, after his father's death. He studied at his tribe's school, and then at Rawdat al-Ma'aref School, in Jerusalem. He later entered the nationalist Rawda College in Jerusalem. He took part in the revolt of 1936-39, and afterward fled to Egypt. In 1945, he became one of the leaders of the Palestine Arab Party, and in 1946, he was among the organisers and founders of the Arab Conference for Tribes and Villages. In 1947 and 1948, he collaborated with Abd al-Qader al-Husseiny in organising the semi-regular *al-Jehad al-Muqaddas* Palestinian forces. He was a member of their National Committee in Beersheba, and the Arab Higher Committee appointed him commander of the forces in the Beersheba area. In early 1948, he actively participated in operations against Jewish settlements, and in April 1948 was among those who greeted and accompanied the Muslim Brotherhood forces from Egypt who had come to fight in Palestine. After the 1948 war, Sheikh Abu-Sitta, with most of his tribe, expelled to the Gaza Strip, although several families from the tribe were expelled to Jordan (Abu-Khusa 1994: 129-130; Shavit et al. 1983: 13; Abu-Sitta 1995: 18).

According to the Ma'in Abu-Sitta Society (1994), Abdalla Musa Abu-Sitta he devoted all his life to the liberty of his country, Palestine. A leader in the rebellion of 1936, commanded volunteers from Khan Yunis, Gaza, and Hebron. They blew up British trains, attacked their convoys, and occupied Beersheba in the summer of 1938. The occupation lasted for one year. He joined the Youth Party (*al-Shabab*) and was a political refugee in Egypt from 1939 to the early forties. He returned to Palestine, re-formed his group of fighters, and established a defence committee for Beersheba. He worked with the Muslim Brotherhood, and with Abd al-Qader al-Husseiny. He formed *Feday'iin* groups (soldiers prepared to sacrifice their lives) and the first political organization for the refugees. He became a deputy in the Legislative Council in Gaza, represented Palestine in several international forums, and was the first Palestine Ambassador to Qatar. He left all this to mobilize forces in Jordan. Because of his influence among Jordan's sheikhs, he was assassinated by the Jordanian Army in 1970 (Ma'in Abu-Sitta Society 1994).

Abd al-Razek Hammad Abu-Sitta

According to the official account of the Ma'in Abu-Sitta Society (1994), Abd al-Razek Hammad Abu-Sitta was a literary man, a speaker, and an ardent nationalist. He formed the Arab Bedouin Society in Beersheba in 1936. Although his resources were meagre, he rented a house for the society; it was a club, meeting place, and guesthouse for sheikhs. He called for active patriotism and issued warnings to traitors who arranged land sales to Jews, carrying the skull of a dead camel for emphasis!. He made tours among clans, accompanied by al-Azhar preachers. In 1936, he demanded that the British be evacuated from Palestine, for which he was imprisoned in Acre for six months. In 1946, he held a conference in Ma'in Abu-Sitta, attended by notables from Khan Yunis and Gaza calling for Palestinian independence.

Hajj Mahmud Saqr Abu-Sitta

According to the official account of the Ma'in Abu-Sitta Society (1994), Mahmud Saqr Abu-Sitta took great care in preserving the land of Ma'in Abu-Sitta and increased his holdings in the south and west, up to 'Abasan, whose borders he respected. His sons were Mhammad, a surgeon, and the celebrated Hamed, a civil engineer. He devoted 40 years of his life to the selfless and persistent pursuit of national aspirations.

Ghawaly Abu al-Hussain

Sheikh 'Abd-Rabba Subh Abu al-Hussain was sheikh of the Ghawaly Abu al-Hussain tribe during the British Mandate (al-'Aref 1933: 44; 1934: 82-89). After the 1948 war, the whole tribe was expelled to the Gaza Strip (Abu-Khusa 1994: 131; IDF 1954: 15). According to Bailey (1981: 48), the distribution of tribal members in 1981 was as follows: Deir al-Balah region 500; Khan Yunis refugee camp, 180; Khan Yunis region, 40; Rafah region,170; Rafah refugee camp, 50. Bailey, also tell us that the Abu-Mgheisib sub-tribe was distributed as follows: at the Khan Yunis refugees camp, 112; Deir al-Balah region, 235; Deir al-Balah refugee camp, 100.

Ghawaly Abu-Shalhub

Sheikh Salem Salman Abu-Shalhub was leader of the Ghawaly Abu-Shalhub tribe (al-'Aref 1933: 44; 1934: 82-89). After the 1948 war, the tribe was expelled to the Gaza Strip (Abu-Khusa 1994: 131; IDF 1954: 15). According to Bailey (1981), their distribution in 1981 was as follows: Deir al-Balah refugee camp, 4; Khan Yunis, 191; Rafah refugee camp, 190.

Ghawaly Abu-Khatla

Sheikh Isma'il Hamed Abu-Khatla was the tribe's leader during the British Mandate (al-'Aref 1933: 44; 1934: 82-89). After the 1948 war, Sheikh Ziadeh Isma'il Hamed Abu-Khatla and almost all of his tribe were expelled to the Gaza Strip; the remainder, mainly Abu-Kharma, were expelled to Jordan with Sheikh Salameh Salem Abu-Kharma, who was succeeded by his son Sheikh Mhammad Salameh Salem Abu-Kharma (Abu-Khusa 1994: 132-133 ; IDF 1954: 15). According to Bailey (1981: 48), their distribution in 1981 was thus: Deir al-Balah refugee camp, 4; Khan Yunis refugee camp, 18; Rafah refugee camp, 131.

Ghawaly Abu-Bakra

The tribe's sheikh during the Mandate was Jum'ah Mhammad Abu-Bakra (al-'Aref 1933: 44; 1934: 82-89). After the 1948 war, they were expelled to the Gaza Strip (Abu-Khusa 1994:131; IDF 1954: 15). According to Bailey (1981: 48), their distribution as of 1981 was thus: Deir al-Balah refugee camp, 45; Rafah refugee camp, 139.

Ghawaly Abu-'Amra

The tribe's sheikh during the Mandate was Salameh Selim Abu-'Amra (al-'Aref 1933: 44; 1934: 82-89), who was succeeded by Sheikh 'Ayyad 'Atta Abu-'Amra. After the 1948 war, part of the tribe was expelled to the Gaza Strip with Sheikh 'Ayyad 'Atta Abu-'Amra (Abu-Khusa 1994: 136). Most members of the tribe were expelled to Jordan with Sheikh Ahmad 'Abdalla Abu-'Amra. Another small part, 42 souls in all, stayed in the Negev under Sheikh Ihlaiyel Abu-'Amra, who served in the police during the British Mandate (IDF 1954: 15, 28). According to Bailey (1981: 48), the tribe's distribution as of 1981 was as follows: Deir al-Balah region, 630; Rafah refugee camp, 414.

Ghawaly al-Zurei'y

The tribe's sheikh during the Mandate was 'Abd al-Karim Ahmad al-Zurei'y (al-'Aref 1933: 44; 1934: 82-89). After the 1948 war, the tribe was expelled to the Gaza Strip (IDF 1954: 15). Some of the tribe stayed in the Negev, living in the midst of other tribes (Abu-Khusa 1994: 128). According to Bailey (1981: 48), their distribution as of 1981 was as follows: Deir al-Balah region, 400; Dir al-Balah refugee camp, 170; Khan Yunis refugee camp, 202.

Ghawaly al-'Umur

The tribe's sheikh during the Mandate was 'Amira Salem al-'Umur (al-'Aref 1933: 44; 1934: 82-89). After the 1948 war, the tribe was expelled to the Gaza Strip (Abu-Khusa 1994: 132; IDF 1954: 15).

Ghawaly al-Naba'at

The tribe's sheikh during the Mandate was Mesleh Selim Ibn-Jarmy (al-'Aref 1933: 44; 1934: 82-87). After the 1948 war, the tribe was expelled to the Gaza Strip (Abu-Khusa 1994: 135). According to Bailey (1981: 49), their distribution as of 1981 was as follows: Khan Yunis region, 475; Rafah refugee camp, 400.

Ghawaly Abu-'Uwayly

According to Bailey (1981: 49), the tribe's distribution as of 1981 was as follows: Deir al-Balah region, 170; Deir al-Balah refugee camp, 20; Khan Yunis refugee camp, 200; Rafah region, 40; Rafah refugee camp, 40.

Wuhaydat Tarabin

The tribe's sheikh during the Mandate was Hasan Nemr al-Wuhaydy (al-'Aref 1933: 44; 1934: 90). After the 1948 war, Sheikh Hasan Abu-Nemr al-Wuhaydy and the tribe were expelled to the Gaza Strip, although a few families were expelled to Jordan (Abu-Khusa 1994: 143; IDF 1954: 16). According to Bailey (1981: 49), their distribution as of 1981 was as follows: Jabalya refugee camp, 290; Deir al-Balah refugee camp, 390; Gaza City, 150.

Hasanat Abu Mu'eileq

The tribe's sheikh during the Mandate was Musa Salem Abu-Mu'eileq (al-'Aref 1933: 44; 1934: 88-90), who was succeeded by his son Kamel. After the 1948 war, Sheikh Kamel Musa Abu-Mu'eileq and the tribe were expelled to the Gaza Strip (Abu-Khusa 1994: 143; Abu-Mu'eileq 1990: 80; IDF 1954: 16).

Jarawin Abu-Ghalyun

The tribe's sheikh during the Mandate was Sliman Ghayth Abu-Ghalyun (al-'Aref 1933: 44; 1934: 91-93). He studied at his tribe's primary school, then at the Beersheba School. He was one of those sent to the school in Istanbul. Before and during the British Mandate, he served as *mustanteq*, or examining magistrate. His main responsibility in that capacity was to investigate conflicts between tribes and pass on the results of his investigations on to the Qaima-qam and chief of police, at their offices in the Saraya House in Beer-sheba. He was subsequently appointed sheikh of his tribe and judge of the Tribal Court in Beersheba (al-'Aref 1933: 62-69), eventually being succeeded by his son, Sheikh Hammad, who was succeeded by his son, Sheikh Selim. After the1948 war, Sheikh Sliman Ghayth Abu-Ghalyun and most of his tribe were expelled to Jordan, although some of them stayed in the Negev (Abu-Khusa 1994: 150-151; IDF 1954: 15).

Jarawin Abu-Yehya

The tribe's sheikh during the Mandate was Farhan Sliman Abu-Yehya (al-'Aref 1933: 44; 1934: 91-93). He was succeeded by his son, Sheikh 'Attiya. After the 1948 war, Sheikh 'Attiya Farhan Abu-Yehya and his tribe were expelled to Jordan (Abu-Khusa 1994: 152; IDF 1954: 16).

Jarawin Abu-S'eilik

The tribe's sheikh during the Mandate was Mansur 'Iyd Abu-S'eilik (al-'Aref 1933: 44; 1934: 91-93), who was succeeded by his son Sheikh Kasem. After the 1948 war, Sheikh Kasem Mansur Abu-S'eilik and most of his tribe were expelled to Jordan; Sheikh Kasem was succeeded by his son, Sheikh 'Iyd Kasem. Another part of the tribe called Abu-Srayhan was expelled to Jordan with the current sheikh, Selim Msallam Abu-Srayhan; the other part of Abu-Sray-han, with their families, stayed in the Negev, composing a new tribe of 145 souls under Sheikh Jabr Abu-Srayhan (Abu-Khusa 1994: 151; IDF 1954: 16, 28). Sheikh Jabr was succeeded by his son, Sheikh 'Awda Jabr Abu-Srayhan.

'Azazma

According to Israeli estimates (IDF 1954: 20), the 'Azazma clan numbered some 12,000 (Marx 1967: 11). According to al-Dabbagh (1991: 455), in 1931 they numbered 8,678 (4,053 males, 4,025 females), and in the summer of 1946 they numbered 16,370. Con-cerning the expulsion of the al-'Azazma clan from the Negev, see Benny Morris (1996:178-82), and Rosalyn Higgins (1969:147-49).

Mhemdiyin

The tribe's sheikh during the Mandate was 'Awda Sliman Abu-Jkhaydem (al-'Aref 1933: 45; 1934: 94-102). After the 1948 war, the sheikh, with one part of his tribe, was expelled to Jordan; he was succeeded by his son, Sheikh Mhammad 'Awda Abu-Jkhaydem. Another part of the tribe was expelled to the Gaza Strip and Sinai. A third part stayed in the Negev amongst the 'Azazma tribe (Abu-Khusa 1994: 159; IDF 1954: 21).

Subhiyeen

The tribe's sheikh during the Mandate was Sallam 'Iyd Ibn-Krayshan (al-'Aref 1933: 45; 1934: 94-102). After the 1948 war, Sheikh Msallam Krayshan and his tribe were expelled to Jordan (IDF 1954: 21). The current sheikh is Farajalla Farraaj Abu-Ras, who served in the Jordanian security forces (Abu-Khusa 1994:161).

Sbayhat

The tribe's sheikh during the Mandate was Salem Msallam Abu-Samra, who was succeeded by Sheikh Hajj Sliman Abu-Samra (al-'Aref 1933: 45; 1934: 94-102). After the 1948 war, Sheikh Hajj Sliman Abu-Samra and his tribe were expelled to Jordan; a small part of the tribe stayed in the Negev (Abu-Khusa 1994: 162; IDF 1954: 21).

Zaraba

The tribe's sheikh during the mandate was 'Iyd Suweilem Ibn-Rebi'eh (al-'Aref 1933: 45; 1934: 94-102), who was succeeded by his son, Sheikh Suweilem. After the 1948 war, the tribe was expelled to Jordan (IDF 1954: 21). In Jordan, one branch of the tribe divided and became the al-Batatrch tribe, headed by Sheikh Salem Abu-Qbayleh, who was succeeded by his son, Sheikh Salameh Salem Abu-Qbayleh, who served as an officer in the Jordanian Army. According to Abu-Khusa (1994: 163), part of the al-Batatreh stayed in the Negev after the 1948 war.

Farahin

The tribe's sheikh during the Mandate was 'Ali Msallam Ibn-Khadira (al-'Aref 1933: 45; 1934: 94-102), who was succeeded by his brother, Sheikh 'Iyd Msallam Ibn-Khadira, who in turn was succeeded by his son, Sheikh 'Ali 'Iyd Ibn-Khadira. After the 1948 war, the sheikh and his tribe were expelled to Jordan. The current sheikh is Mhammad 'Ali 'Iyd Ibn-Khadira (Abu-Khusa 1994: 165; IDF 1954: 20).

Mas'udin

The tribe's sheikh during the Mandate was Salameh Msallam Ibn-Sa'id (al-'Aref 1933: 45; 1934: 94-102). After the 1948 war, part of the tribe, with the Sheikh Hammad Ibn-Sa'id, was expelled to Jordan, while another part stayed in the Negev under a new sheikh, 'Awda Mansur Abu-M'ammar. The new tribe, called Mas'udin al-'Azazma, numbered 756 (Abu-Khusa 1994: 158; IDF 1954: 21, 28).

Abu-Sakhneh

The tribe's sheikh during the Mandate was 'Awda 'Awwad Abu al-Khayl (al-'Aref 1933: 45; 1934: 94-102), who was succeeded by his son, Sheikh Naser, who in turn was succeeded by his son, Sheikh Farhan. After the 1948 war, Sheikh Farhan Naser Abu al-Khayl and his tribe were expelled to Jordan (Abu-Khusa 1994: 164; IDF 1954: 21).

'Assyiat

The tribe's sheikh during the Mandate was Sliman Salman al-Nmily (al-'Aref 1933: 45; 1934: 94-102). After the 1948 war, Sheikh Selim Abu-Nuirah and his tribe were expelled to Jordan, where he was eventually succeeded by Sheikh Salem Sliman al-Nmily. A small part of the tribe stayed in the Negev amongst the al-'Azazma tribe (Abu-Khusa 1994: 162; IDF 1954: 21).

Mray'at

The tribe's sheikh during the Mandate was Salem Suweilem al-Azraq (al-'Aref 1933: 45; 1934: 94-102). After the 1948 war, Sheikh Suweilem al-Azraq and his tribe were expelled to Jordan. Sheikh Suweilem was succeeded by Sheikh 'Iyd Mhaysen al-Huly. A small part of the tribe stayed in the Negev amongst the al-'Azazma tribe (Abu-Khusa 1994: 160; IDF 1954: 21).

Sarahin

During the Mandate the Sarahin had two tribes or sub-tribes (al-'Aref 1933: 45; 1934: 94-102; IDF 1954: 20) the Sarahin Ibn-Sa'd, headed by Sheikh Selim Ibn-Sa'd, and the Sarahin al-Atim, headed by Sheikh Salem al-Atim. The current sheikh is Sa'd Ibn-Sa'id al-Atim (Abu-Khusa 1994: 165). After the 1948 war, some of the Sarahin stayed in the Negev amongst the al-'Azazma tribe, while other parts were expelled to Jordan and Sinai (Abu-Khusa 1994: 165; Higgins 1969: 147-149; IDF 1954: 20).

Riattyia

After the 1948 war, Sheikh Mhammad al-Riatty and most of his tribe were expelled to Jordan; the current sheikh is 'Abdalla Hasan al-Riatty. One part of the tribe was expelled to the Gaza Strip, while another, smaller part stayed amongst the al-'Azazma tribe in the Negev (Abu-Khusa 1994: 167; al-'Aref 1934: 101-102; IDF 1954: 21).

The Riattyia used to dwell several months a year in stone houses. They maintained religious schools divided into 'forms'. They highly intelligent, emphasise education, and were inclined towards religious zealotry. They were often employed as preachers (*khatibs*) with the Bedouin (Bresslavsky 1946: 264-65).

Abu-Samhadaneh

After the 1948 war, Sheikh Salman Abu-Samhadaneh and his tribe were expelled to the Gaza Strip, near Khan Yunis (IDF 1954: 21).

Sattary

After the 1948 war, Sheikh Hajj 'Abdalla al-Sattary and his tribe were expelled to Jordan (IDF 1954: 21).

Tiyaha

According to Israeli estimates (IDF 1954: 17), the Tiyaha numbered some 18,000 (Marx 1967: 11). According to al-Dabbagh (1991: 434), in 1931 they numbered about 13,708 (7,507 males, 6,201 females), and in the summer of 1946, some 25,153. It should be noted that was included in these estimations the Dhullam clan. According to Bailey (1981: 50), the Tiyaha refugees in the Gaza Strip numbered 2,000 in 1981.

Hukuk al-Huzaiyil

The tribe's sheikh during the Mandate was Salman 'Ali al-Huzaiyil. He was also a tribal judge during the British Mandate (al-'Aref

1933: 45, 68; 1934: 105-108). After the 1948 war, the sheikh stayed in the Negev with his tribe, who numbered 1,573. He was a very respected and influential figure among the Bedouin. He was a specialist in traditional Bedouin medicine, especially in treating sciatica (*'irq al-nsi /nisa*) by cauterization using the dried leaves phagnalon plant (Phagnalon rupestre: *qadeh, sufan*), which grew on rocky ground. People from all over the country, and even from abroad, would come to him for treatment. He gave his sons an education, and several of them served in the police during the Mandatory period, most notably his sons Jaddu' and Salameh (Abu-Khusa 1994: 97; Abu-Rabi'a 1983: 1-30 ;IDF 1954: 18, 23-24). After his death, he was succeeded by his son Jaddu', who was in turn succeeded by his brother Salameh, who died in 1997.

Hukuk al-Asad

The tribe's sheikh during the Mandate was Sliman Selim al-Asad. He was succeeded by his son, Sheikh Khalil, who in turn was succeeded by Sheikh Fa'ur al-Asad. After the 1948 war, he and his tribe, a total of 197 persons, stayed in the Negev (Abu-Khusa 1994: 98, al-'Aref 1933: 45; 1934: 105-108; IDF 1954: 18, 24). After Sheikh Fa'ur's death, he was succeeded by his son 'Ali.

Hukuk al-Brayqy

The tribe's sheikh during the Mandate was Selim 'Ali al-Brayqy (al-'Aref 1933: 45; 1934: 105-108). He was succeeded by Sheikh Salem Selim al-Brayqy. After the 1948 war, the sheikh and some of his tribe were expelled to Jordan, while part of the tribe stayed in the Negev. After Sheikh Salem's death, he was succeeded by his son, Sheikh Su'ud Salem Selim al-Brayqy, the current sheikh (Abu-Khusa 1994: 99; IDF 1954: 18). According to Bailey (1981: 50), in 1981, there were some 1,700 al-Brayqy living in the Nuseirat refugee camp, they apparently were expelled to the Gaza Strip after the 1948 war.

Hukuk Abu-'Abdun

The tribe's sheikh during the Mandate was 'Ideisan Hasan Abu-'Abdun (al-'Aref 1933: 45; 1934: 105-108). After the 1948 war, Sheikh Ibrahim Abu-'Abdun and one part of the tribe were expelled to Jordan; another part was expelled to the Gaza Strip. A third part, which stayed in the Negev with Sheikh Hasan Abu-'Abdun, numbered 128 (IDF 1954: 18, 24-25). The current sheikh is 'Ideisan Hasan Abu-'Abdun.

Hukuk al-Hamamdeh

The tribe's sheikh during the British Mandate was Hasan Juma'h al-Franjy, who came to power in1940. After the 1948 war, the sheikh and his tribe were expelled to the Gaza Strip (Abu-Khusa 1994: 98-99; IDF 1954: 18).

Bili

The tribe's sheikh in 1920 was Ihlaiyil Salameh al-Sahabin (al-'Aref 1933: 45; 1934: 114-115). He was succeeded by Sheikh Mhammad Mas'ad al-Herfy. After the 1948 war, one part of the tribe was expelled to the Gaza Strip, while the sheikh and another part of the tribe were expelled to East Hallabat, between al-Zarqa and al-Azraq, in Jordan. There the Bili tribe divided to produce another new tribe, Qrinat Bili, headed by Sheikh Salem al-Habanin al-Balawy (Abu-Khusa 1994: 121-122; IDF 1954: 19).

'Alamat Abu-Labbeh

The tribe's sheikh during the Mandate was Salameh Muhsen Abu-Labbeh. He was succeeded by his son, Sheikh Muhsen, who was succeeded by Sheikh al-Qaisy Abu-Labbeh. After the latter's death, he was succeeded by his son, Sheikh Kamel al-Qaisy Abu-Labbeh, the current sheikh. After the 1948 war, the sheikh and his tribe were expelled to Jordan (Abu-Khusa 1994: 95-96; al-'Aref 1933: 45; 1934: 108-109; IDF 1954: 18).

'Alamat Abu-Shunnar

When the British conquered the Negev, the sheikh of all al-'Alamat tribes was Salameh Musa Abu-Shunnar. The British authorities put him under arrest, after which the al-'Alamat divided into three tribes: Abu-Labbeh, Abu-Shunnar, and Abu-Jqaym.

Sheikh Musa Hasan Abu-Shunnar was the tribe's sheikh during the British Mandate. After the 1948 war, part of the tribe stayed in the Negev, while the other part was expelled to Jordan with Sheikh Mhammad Salameh Abu-Shunnar (Abu-Khusa 1994: 95-96; al-'Aref 1933: 45; 1934: 108-109). According to Bailey (1981: 51), in 1981 about ten members of the tribe lived in the Jabalya refugee camp.

'Alamat Abu-Jqaym

The tribe's sheikh during the Mandate was 'Atta Salem Abu-Jqaym. After the 1948 war, the sheikh and his tribe were expelled to Jordan (Abu-Khusa 1994: 95-96; al-'Aref 1933: 45; 1934: 108-109; IDF 1954: 18).

Shlaliyin

The tribe's sheikh during the Mandate was Mhammad Jum'ah Abu-Ghayth (who came to power in 1920), who was succeeded by his son, Sheikh Salameh, also during the British Mandate (al-'Aref 1933: 45; 1934: 115-116). After the 1948 war, the sheikh and most of his tribe were expelled to Jordan. After his death, he was succeeded by his son, Sheikh Musa, who died in 1994; his brother, Sheikh Ghayth Salameh Mhammad Abu-Ghayth, then became sheikh. Musa and his brother Ghayth were among the leaders of the PLO (Abu-Khusa 1994: 107-108). Another part of the tribe, numbering 165, stayed in the Negev amongst the tribe of Sheikh Mhammad al-Afinesh (IDF 1954: 27). Subsequent sheikhs were his son, Sliman, and his son, 'Izzat Sliman al-Afinesh, who is the current sheikh.

al-Talalqeh

The al-Talalqeh tribe was part of the al-'Atawna tribe before 1948. Sheikh 'Amer al-Talalqeh became a sheikh after the 1948 war, and with most of the tribe (318 persons), he stayed in the Negev (IDF 1954: 26). According to Morris (1996: 249), the tribe was attacked by Israeli forces on 24 May 1953. Two women and one old man were killed, and two children were wounded.

According to Abu-Khusa (1994: 113) the tribe's sheikh during the British mandate was Mhammad Hsein al-Talalqeh; his successor was Sheikh 'Amer Hsein al-Talalqeh, who was killed by Israeli forces in 1956. But according to Negev Bedouin sources, Sheikh 'Amer was arrested by the Israeli Security Intelligence Forces in 1956, under suspicion of collaborating with Egyptian Intelligence Colonel Mustafa Hafez, in Gaza. He was brutally tortured and died in a military hospital. Only after ten years, was he succeeded by his son, Sheikh Salameh 'Amer al-Talalqeh.

It should be noted that Israeli secret forces assassinated Colonel Mustafa Hafez by a letter bomb in Gaza, on 11 July 1956 (Morris 1996: 408-409).

Part of the tribe was expelled to Jordan after the 1948 war, constituting a new tribe, currently under Sheikh Majed Hassan al-Talalqeh (Abu-Khusa 1994: 113).

Qudeirat Abu-Irqaiyiq

The tribe's sheikh during the Mandate was Hajj Harb Salameh Abu-Irqaiyiq (al-'Aref 1933: 46; 1934: 121-25). As a result of the 1948 war, the sheikh and part of his tribe were expelled to Jordan in 1950. Most of the tribe (1,630 persons) stayed in the Negev under Sheikh 'Awadh Ibrahim Abu-Irqaiyiq (IDF 1954: 1-30; Abu-Khusa 1994: 106). Sheikh Hajj Harb was succeeded by Sheikh Ibrahim 'Iyd Abu-Irqaiyiq, who in turn was succeeded by Sheikh Hasan Ibrahim Abu-Irqaiyiq. The current sheikh is Ibrahim Salameh Abu-Irqaiyiq, an educated and charming person.

According to Bailey (1981: 51), about seventy members of the al-Khurtty family from the Abu-Irqayiq tribe were living in the Nuseirat refugee camp in 1981.

Qudeirat al-Sane' (Matarqiya)

The tribe's sheikh during the Mandate was Ibrahim Mhammad al-Sane'. He studied at his tribe's primary school, and continued in the Beersheba school. According to oral interviews with his sons Hajj Hasan al-Sane' (2 July 1998) and Nabhan al-Sane' (16 January 1999, personal communication), he was one of the students who were sent to the school at Istanbul. He became a Hajj, and was the sheikh of his tribe, Qudeirat al-Sane', from 1927 until his death in 1952.

Sheikh Ibrahim was one of the outstanding figures among the Negev Bedouin in the British Mandatory period. He served as a member of the district council in Beersheba, and as a tribal judge (al-'Aref 1934: 245; IDF 1954: 25). He was an avowed and implacable hater of Israel, and co-operated with Egypt in the 1948 war between Israel and Arabs in Palestine (IDF 1954: 25).

During the disturbances of 1929, and even more so in those of 1936-39, Beersheba was a focal point of Arab nationalism. It was here that the ideas of a separate Arab entity and a political and military struggle were born and disseminated amongst the Bedouin. Two major disseminators of Arab nationalism were the Beersheba sheikhs Hamd al-Sane' and Ibrahim al-Sane'; as early as the 1930s, they were mentioned as representatives of the Arab Committee of Palestine in the city of Beersheba. In 1937, Grand Mufti Hajj Amin al-Husseiny held a meeting of all Negev sheikhs in the home of Hajj Ibrahim al-Sane' to co-ordinate strategy against the Jewish settlers in Palestine. On another occasion, Hajj Ibrahim, whose nationalist activities led the Mufti to call him *al-Saleh*, al-Sane' the Righteous, circulated a written pledge not to sell land to the Jews, which many other sheikhs signed. In the possession of Sason Bar-Zvi is a document, signed by eleven Negev Bedouin sheikhs, undertaking to cut off from their tribes not only anyone who sold land to Jews, but any who even served as middleman or agent in any land transfer to Jews. It is worth noting that land sales to Jews continued, although quietly and by means of various stratagems. In order to prevent Bedouin lands from falling into the hands of the Jews, Arab nationalists established a fund, *Sanduq al-Umma*, the National Fund. Moneys for the fund were obtained from Bedouin contributions, as well as from a tax on the sale of livestock and cattle at the Bedouin market in Beersheba. Some of Beersheba's Bedouin, among them Hajj Ibrahim al-Sane', joined the Egyptian forces in the 1948 war between Jews and Arabs and took part in the defense of the city of Beersheba, which was captured by the Israeli Defense Forces on 21 October 1948 (Bar-Zvi 1977: 1-13; Danin and Shimoni 1981: 114-115; Gal-Pe'er 1979a: 284; al-Ghury 1972: 215).

In the 1948 war, the Qudeirat al-Sane' tribe was divided: One part was expelled to the Gaza Strip, but most of the tribe 826 persons under Sheikh Hajj Ibrahim al-Sane' were forced by the Israeli Defense Forces to leave their lands and move to Laqiya, north east of Beersheba, where they stayed for about three years. The Israeli Defense Forces then told them that Israel was going to establish a Jewish settlement at Laqiya, and that their tribe would have to move to Tel-Arad. The sheikh refused to accept the Israeli order and on 17 September 1952, the tribe, with over 100 families (nearly 1,000 persons) was expelled to Jordan, south of Hebron. The Jordanian authorities asked a UN armistice team to return them to Israel. On 26 October 1952, the al-Sane' tribe returned to Israel; seventeen members of the tribe vanished deeper into Jordan and the search for them was not pressed. The tribe crossed back into Israel under their Sheikh Ibrahim, and was forced to move to the Tel-Arad lands, near the Abu-Rabi'a tribe, which helped them during their difficult times. Sheikh Ibrahim was visibly under great strain and his eyes reflected defeat, but he was seen as a leader of a proud people. Three weeks later, in November 1952, Sheikh Hajj

Ibrahim al-Sane' died of a heart attack at Tel-Arad. His sudden death shook the sheikhs and Bedouin tribes and they announced forty days of mourning. Upon Sheikh Hajj Ibrahim's death, his brother Mansur became head of the tribe (Abu-Khusa 1994: 104; Encyc. Palest. Vol.III, 545, Vol.V, 33; Hutchison 1956: 30-38; IDF 1954: 25; Morris 1996: 181-182 ; Hajj Hasan Ibrahim al-Sane', 2 July 1998, personal communication), and he was eventually succeeded by Hajj Sheikh Hasan Ibrahim al-sane'. The present-day Knesset member Talab al-Sane' is the son of 'Amer, brother of Ibrahim and Mansur.

It should be noted that during the 1956 war that pitted Israel, the UK, and France against Egypt, Khalil, the son of Sheikh Hajj Ibrahim escaped to Jordan because the Israeli Security Forces, which suspected him of having "relations" with the Egyptians, wanted to put him in prison ('Alayian and Nabhan al-Sane': 16 January 1999, personal communication). Later he was appointed the sheikh of the al-Sane' tribe in Irbed, Jordan. He died in 1996.

According to Bailey (1981: 51), about seventy members of the Abu-Khubbayzeh family from the Qudeirat al-Sane' tribe, were living in the Nuseirat refugee camp in 1981.

Qudeirat Abu-Kaff (Hrayzat)

Sheikh Hsein Sallam Abu-Kaff served as a Beersheba mayor during the British Mandate. His son Mhemmed succeeded him as sheikh of the tribe. After the 1948 war, the sheikh and most of his tribe were expelled to Jordan. A small part stayed in the Negev amongst the Abu-Irqaiyiq tribe (al-'Aref 1933: 46; 1934: 121-125; IDF 1954: 17). The section of the tribe in Jordan was under Sheikh 'Abd al-Rahman Hsein Abu-Kaff (Abu-Khusa 1994: 105). Those who stayed in the Negev later became an independent tribe under Sheikh Mhammad Jabr Abu-Kaff until his death in 1998. He was succeeded by his son, Jabr Mhammad Jabr Abu-Kaff.

Qudeirat al-'Asam ('Atham)

The tribe's sheikh during the Mandate was Jaddu' Hassan al-'Asam, who was succeeded by Sheikh Mhammad Hassan al-'Asam, also during the British Mandate. After the 1948 war, certain families were expelled to Jordan, but most of the tribe, 735 persons, stayed in the Negev with their sheikh (Abu-Khusa 1994: 106; al-'Aref 1933: 46; 1934: 121-125; IDF 1954: 17, 26), who was a respected sheikh and judge among the Bedouin. The current Sheikh is Salman Mhammad al-'Asam.

Qudeirat al-Hawashleh

The tribe's sheikh during the Mandate was Salameh Jum'ah al-Hawashleh. After the 1948 war, most of the tribe was expelled to Jordan. The sheikh and another part of the tribe stayed in the Negev, amongst the Abu-Irqaiyiq tribe (IDF 1954: 18). They later separated and became an independent tribe under sheikh Hammad Salameh al-Hawashleh.

Ramadin Masamreh

The tribe's sheikh during the Mandate was Hasan Ibrahim al-Masamreh who came to power in 1925 (al-'Aref 1933: 46; 1934: 129-130). After the 1948 war, some members of the tribe were expelled to Gaza and Egypt (IDF 1954: 19). The current sheikh is Serhan Sliman Ibn-Ghayyadh (Abu-Khusa 1994: 110).

Ramadin Shu'ur

The tribe's sheikh during the Mandate was Salameh Ibrahim al-Shu'ur who came to power in 1925 (al-'Aref 1933: 46; 1934: 129-130). After the 1948 war, one part of the tribe, with Sheikh Khalil Ibn-Frayj, was expelled to the West Bank of the Jordan, while another was expelled to Gaza and Egypt (IDF 1954: 19). According to Abu-Khusa (1994: 110), the current sheikhs are: Sheikh Musa Salameh al-Shu'ur, for Ramadin al-Shu'ur; Sheikh Serhan Sliman Ibn-Ghayyadh, for Ramadin Ibn-Ghayyadh; Sheikh Mhammad Khalil al-Frayjat, for Ramadin al-Frayjat.

Bani 'Uqba (al-'Uqby):

The tribe's sheikh during the Mandate was Hajj Mhammad Salem al-'Uqby, who took power in 1920 (al-'Aref 1933: 46; 1934: 116-20). Who was succeeded by his son, Sheikh Ibrahim, who was sheikh until the 1948 war. The sheikh and part of his tribe were then expelled to the Gaza Strip. Another part of the tribe was expelled to Jordan under Sheikh Hajj Ahmad Mhammad al-'Uqby, who was succeeded by his son, Sheikh Majed.

A third part of the tribe, numbering 383, stayed in the Negev, under Sheikh Sliman Mhammad al-'Uqby (Abu-Khusa 1994: 111-112; IDF 1954: 19, 27). Al-'Uqby sheikhs have been very respected judges among the Bedouin, mainly dealing with matrimony and women's issues.

According to Bailey (1981: 51), in 1981 there were about twenty al-'Uqby living at the Nuseirat refugee camp.

Ntush al-'Atawna

The tribe's sheikh during the Mandate was Hasan 'Ali al-'Atawna, who succeeded his father 'Ali in 1920 (al-'Aref 1933: 46; 1934: 111-114). After the 1948 war, the sheikh and part of the tribe were expelled to Jordan. His son 'Izzat served the Jordanian authorities as an advisor on Bedouin affairs. The other part of the tribe, numbering 187, stayed in the Negev with the son of Sheikh Hasan, Sheikh Musa, a highly educated person. The current sheikh in Jordan is Sliman Hsein al-'Atawna (Abu-Khusa 1994:108-109; IDF 1954: 18, 26). According to Bailey (1981: 50), in 1981, about twenty members of the tribe lived in the Nuseirat and Jabalya refugee camps.

'Ayal 'Amry: Rawashdeh

The tribe's sheikh during the Mandate was Sliman Darwish Abu-Rashed (al-'Aref 1933: 46; 1934: 104-11), who was succeeded during the Mandate by Sheikh Musa Sliman Abu-Rashed. After the 1948 war, the sheikh, with most of his tribe, was expelled to the Gaza Strip; the other part of the tribe was deported to the Sinai. After the 1967 war, the sheikh and his tribe were again expelled, this time to Jordan. After his death, he was succeeded by his son, Sheikh Maher Musa Abu-Rashed (Abu-Khusa 1994: 101; IDF 1954: 19).

'Ayal 'Amry: al-'Urur

The tribe's sheikh during the Mandate was Selim Salman al-'Irr (al-'Aref 1933: 46; 1934: 104-111). After the 1948 war, Sheikh Sliman al-'Irr and most of his tribe were expelled to the Gaza Strip. Another part was expelled to Jordan, with Sheikh 'Ali Mhammad al-'Irr. A small group stayed in the Negev (Abu-Khusa 1994: 100; IDF 1954: 19). According to Bailey (1981: 51), in 1981, about 140 al-'Urur tribesmen were living in the Nuseirat refugee camp.

Bdinat

The tribe's sheikh during the Mandate was 'Attiya Salameh Ibn-Khattab. After his death in 1934 (al-'Aref 1933: 46; 1934: 133), he was succeeded by Sheikh Salman Slayyim al-Mraby (Abu-Khusa 1994: 101-102). After the 1948 war, the sheikh and his tribe were expelled to the Gaza Strip (IDF 1954: 18). Mahmud Abdalla al-Mraby subsequently became sheikh (Abu-Khusa 1994: 101-102).

Qalazin Tiyaha

The tribe's sheikh during the Mandate was 'Abdallah Salem Abu-al-Ghusayn, who came to power in 1920. Al-'Aref and Abu-Khusa believe that the Qalazin Tiyaha belong to the Jubarat clan (Abu-Khusa 1994: 112; al-'Aref 1933: 46; 1934: 133). After the 1948 war, part of the tribe was expelled to Jordan, and other part stayed in the Negev amongst other tribes, not as an independent tribe with its own sheikh.

Qatatweh

The tribe's sheikh during the Mandate was Hasan Salem al-Qattawy, later Hajj (Abu-Khusa 1994: 123; al-'Aref 1933: 46; 1934: 132-33). After the 1948 war, Sheikh Mhammad Hasan Abu-'Aydeh and Sheikh Hasan Abu-Yusef were expelled with their tribes to the Gaza Strip and Egypt (IDF 1954: 19).

Dhullam

According to Israeli estimates (IDF 1954: 26-27), the Dhullam clan numbered approximately 4,000 in 1948. The Dhullam, belonged to Bili tribes from Hejaz at Arabia Peninsula, who came to Palestine in the seventeen century (Bailey 1989: 9-21).

Abu-Rabi'a (Ihmisat)

The tribe's sheikh during the Mandate was Salem 'Iyd Abu-Rabi'a, who was succeeded by his son Khalil, who was succeeded by his son, Hajj Salman. Hajj Salman was a famous leader and tribal judge in Palestine, with good relations with the British authorities. He died on 12 April 1946 at a Hospital in Jerusalem. Hajj Salman was succeeded by his uncle 'Ali Khalil until the 1948 war. Sheikh 'Ali and a small part of the tribe emigrated to Jordan, while most of the tribe, 1,632 persons, stayed in the Negev under his brother Sheikh Hammad Khalil Abu-Rabi'a, who was a member of the Knesset (from 1973 to 1977 and 1979 to 1981) until he was murdered by a Druze in 1981.

During his term, he became the leader of the Bedouin throughout the country. After his murder, sheikhs and leaders of the Bedouin and urban Arabs from all over the Middle East came to console his family (Abu-Khusa 1994: 124-25; al-'Aref 1933: 46; 1934: 125-29; IDF 1954: 26-27). He was succeeded by Sheikh Khalil Salman Khalil Abu-Rabi 'a (Sheikh 'Ali Khalil Abu-Rabi'a and Hajj Mhammad Hasan Abu-Rabi'a, 1 February 1998, personal communication).

Abu-Juwei'ed (Lehaybeh)

The tribe's sheikh during the Mandate was Mhaysen Hmeid Abu-Juwei'ed (al-'Aref 1933: 46; 1934: 125-129). He was succeeded by his son, Sheikh Mhemmed; the tribe numbered 873 persons in 1948 (Abu-Khusa 1994: 124-25; IDF 1954: 27). Sheikh Mhemmed was succeeded by his son, Sheikh Khalil.

Abu-Qreinat (Mehanyeh)

The tribe's sheikh during the Mandate was Salameh Sbayh al-Sbayhat (al-'Aref 1933: 46; 1934: 125-29), who was succeeded by Sheikh 'Ali Salman Abu-Qreinat. After the 1948 war, the sheikh and 1,128 of his tribesmen stayed in the Negev (IDF 1954: 26-27). He was succeeded by his son Mhammad. The current sheikh is Sliman Salem Abu-Qreinat.

Janabib

The tribe's sheikh during the Mandate was 'Awda Sa'd al-Keshkher, who was succeeded by Sheikh Salameh al-Keshkher. After the 1948 war, the sheikh stayed in the Negev with two hundred of his tribesmen. He was succeeded by Salem Sliman al-Keshkher (al-'Aref, 1933: 46; 1934: 125-29; Bailey, 1989: 9-21; IDF 1954:18, 26-27; Marx 1967: 13).

Hanajira

In 1931 the population of the Hanajira clan was estimated at 3,735 (2,058 males, 1,677 females). In the summer of 1946, it had reached about 7,125 (al-Dabbagh 1991: 406-12; al-'Aref 1933: 46, 1934:134-39). According to Israeli estimates (IDF 1954: 12), they numbered approximately 7,000. According to Bailey (1981: 51), in 1981 they numbered approximately 10,000 in the Gaza Strip.

Abu-Meddein

The tribe's sheikh during the Mandate was Freih Farhan Abu-Meddein. During the British Mandate he served as a member of the Tribal Court and the Advisory Council to the High Commissioner (1920-22). In 1922, he became a member of the Legislative Council (al-'Aref 1933: 46, 68; 1934: 134-39; Wasserstein 1991: 90, 93, 224; PRO FO 371/5124/149). He was one of the best-known, most influential sheikhs in the Negev. He also served as a mayor of Beersheba in the early 1920s (al-'Aref 1933: 46, 68; 1934: 134-39). After the 1948 war, the sheikh and his tribe were expelled to the Gaza strip (Abu-Khusa 1994: 153-54; IDF 1954: 12; Shavit, Foldstein and Be'er 1983: 12). His grandson and namesake, Freih Mustafa Abu-Meddein, a lawyer, was appointed by Chairman Yaser 'Arafat to be Minister of Justice in the Palestinian Authority.

Dawahra (Abu-Daher)

The tribe's sheikh during the Mandate was Ahmad Abu-Daher (al-'Aref 1933: 46; 1934: 134-39). After the 1948 war, the tribe was expelled to the Gaza Strip (Abu-Khusa 1994: 155; IDF 1954: 12).

al-Smeiry

The tribe's sheikh during the Mandate was Selim 'Abdallah al-Smeiry (al-'Aref 1933: 46; 1934: 134-39), who was succeeded by Sheikh Juma'h al-Smeiry. After the 1948 war, the sheikh and his tribe were expelled to the Gaza Strip (Abu-Khusa 1994: 156; IDF 1954: 12).

Nuseirat

The tribe's sheikh during the Mandate was 'Aaysh Farhan al-Msaddar (al-'Aref 1933: 46; 1934: 134-39), who was succeeded by Sheikh Freih al-Msaddar in the 1940s. In 1946, Sheikh Freih was among the principal figures of Husseiny's Palestine Arab Party in the Beersheba region. He was also a member of the Arab Higher Council for the establishment of a treasury, and of its finance committee. In April 1948, he was among those who greeted the Muslim Brotherhood volunteers from Egypt who came to fight in Palestine (Shavit, Foldstein and Be'er 1983: 323). After the 1948 war, the sheikh and most of his tribe were expelled to the Gaza Strip; other Nuseirat families were expelled to Jordan (IDF 1954: 12). After the 1967 war, some families were deported from the Gaza Strip to Jordan (Abu-Khusa 1994: 154-56).

Jubarat

In 1931 the population of the Jubarat clan was estimated at 4,452 (2,434 males, 2,008 females). In the summer of 1946, it had reached 7,528 (al-Dabbagh 1991: 413). According to Israeli estimates (IDF 1954: 12), they numbered only 5,000 in 1948.

Abu-Jaber

The tribe's sheikh during the Mandate was Hasan Saleh Abu-Jaber. During the British Mandate, he served as a member of the Tribal Court (al-'Aref 1933: 47; 1934: 140-44). After the 1948 war, Sheikh Hasan Saleh Abu-Jaber and part of the tribe were expelled to the Gaza Strip (IDF 1954: 12-13). Another part, including the sheikh's brothers Mhammad and Ahmad, was expelled to Jordan.

Sheikh Hasan Saleh Abu-Jaber was a member of the Palestine National Council before 1967. He had three sons: Dr. Sherif, Hsein, and Fayz. Fayz was educated at Egyptian universities. When the sheikh died in the Gaza Strip, he was succeeded by his son, Sheikh Hsein Hasan Abu-Jaber (Abu-Khusa 1994: 57-58).

Rteimat Abu al-'Udus

The tribe's sheikh during the Mandate was Nemr Hamd Abu al-'Udus, who was succeeded by his son, Sheikh Mhammad Nemr Hamd Abu al-'Udus (al-'Aref 1933: 47; 1934: 140-48). After the 1948 war, the sheikh and his tribe were expelled to Jordan (IDF., 1954: 12-13).Today the sheikh is Ahmad Abu-Khusa, the author of several books about the Negev Bedouin. Sheikh Ahmad also served as a captain (*naqib*) in the Jordanian Army (Abu-Khusa 1994: 61-70).

Rteimat Fuqara al-Masharfeh

The tribe's sheikh during the Mandate was Khalil Hdiwy al-Masharfeh (al-'Aref 1933: 47; 1934: 140-48). After the 1948 war, the sheikh and his tribe were expelled to Jordan (IDF 1954: 12). Sheikh Khalil died in 1980 in Jordan. Today the sheikh is Sherif Mhammad Hdiwy al-Masharfeh (Abu-Khusa 1994: 79).

Qalazin Thawabteh

The tribe's sheikh during the Mandate was Baraka Selim Ibn-Thabet (al-'Aref 1933: 47; 1934: 140-51). After the 1948 war, the sheikh and most of his tribe were expelled to the Gaza Strip (IDF 1954:12-

13). A small part was expelled to Jordan. After the 1967 war, the tribe in the Gaza Strip was expelled to Jordan and reunited with their fellow tribesmen, there since 1948 (Abu-Khusa 1994: 80).

Hasanat Ibn-Sabbah

The tribe's sheikh during the Mandate was Hajj Mhammad Ibn-Sabbah who took power in 1930 (al-'Aref 1933: 47; 1934: 140-50). He was succeeded by Sheikh Hasan Ibn-Sabbah, and then Sheikh 'Umar Salman Ibn-Sabbah, who, after his death, was succeeded by his son, Sheikh Mhammad 'Umar Salman Ibn-Sabbah. It should be noted that the whole tribe was expelled to Jordan after the 1948 war (Abu-Khusa 1994: 71-72; IDF 1954: 12-13).

'Amarin Ibn-'Ajlan

The tribe's sheikh during the Mandate was Sliman Ibn-'Ajlan (al-'Aref 1933: 47; 1934: 140-50). After the 1948 war, the tribe divided into two parts: the 'Amarin Ibn-'Ajlan, who were expelled to the Gaza Strip, and the 'Amarin al-Ra'ay, who were departed to Jordan (IDF 1954: 12-13). According to Abu-Khusa (1994: 77), there were originally two tribes, both of which were expelled to Jordan in 1948: the 'Amarin Ibn-'Ajlan, led by Sheikh Mhammad Ibn-'Ajlan, who was succeeded by Sheikh Sliman Mhammad Ibn-'Ajlan; and the 'Amarin al-Ra'ay, the sheikh of which in 1932 was Sliman al-Ra'ay, who was succeeded by Sheikh Salman al-Ra'ay. Today the sheikh is 'Abd al-Rahman Salman al-Ra'ay. The tribe has many educated notables, including Mr. Mhammad Ahmad al-Amir, a judge at the Court of Appeal in Amman.

Wuhaydat Jubarat

The tribe's sheikh during the Mandate was Hsein Su'ud al-Wuhaydy (al-'Aref 1933: 47; 1934: 140-46). After the 1948 war, the whole tribe was expelled to Jordan, and broke up into two tribes: led by Sheikh 'Abd al-Razzaq Hsein Su'ud al-Wuhaydy and Sheikh Habib al-Wuhaydy, who was succeeded after his death by 'Atta al-Wuhaydy (Abu-Khusa 1994: 81-82; IDF 1954: 12-13).

Sa'adenat al-Nuweiry

The tribe's sheikh during the Mandate was Sliman Mehsen al-Nuweiry (al-'Aref 1933: 47; 1934: 140-53). After the 1948 war, the whole tribe was expelled to Jordan (IDF 1954: 12-13). Today the sheikh is Hasan Sliman al-Nuweiry (Abu-Khusa 1994:74).

Sa'adenat Abu-Jrayban

The tribe's sheikh during the Mandate was Mhammad Salem Abu-Jrayban (al-'Aref 1933: 47; 1934: 140-53). After the 1948 war, the whole tribe was expelled to Jordan (IDF 1954: 12-13). Sheikh Mhammad was succeeded by Sheikh Salameh Abu-Jrayban, who in turn was succeeded by Sheikh Hasan Mhammad Abu-Jrayban (Abu-Khusa 1994: 74).

Deqs

The tribe's sheikh during the Mandate was Hsein 'Iyd al-Deqs. After his death in the 1940s, he was succeeded by his son, Sheikh 'Abd al-Hamid (al-'Aref 1933: 47; 1934: 140-43). After the 1948 war, the whole tribe was expelled to Jordan (IDF 1954: 12-13).

One of the educated notables of the Deqs tribe is Mr. Izhaq Diqs, worked as an elementary school teacher in Jordan and civil servant in Saudi Arabia; he is the author of *A Bedouin Boyhood*. Another prominent tribesman is Dr. Kamel Salameh al-Deqs, instructor of Arabic literature at the King Abd al-'Aziz Al Su'ud University. Dr. Mhammad Abd al-Mawla al-Deqs, is an instructor of sociology at Jordanian University (Abu-Khusa 1994: 73; Diqs 1984: 5-47).

Sawarket Ibn-Rafi'

The tribe's sheikh during the Mandate was Sliman Ibn-Rafi', who served as a member of the first Tribal Council in Beersheba (al-'Aref 1933: 47; 1934: 140-49). After the 1948 war, most of the tribe was expelled to Jordan, and a small part to the Gaza Strip (IDF 1954: 12-13). Today the sheikh is 'Iyd Ibn-Rafi' (Abu-Khusa 1994: 35, 75-76).

Walaydeh

The tribe's sheikh during the Mandate was Sliman Hammad Abu-Sala'eh (al-'Aref 1933: 47; 1934: 140-44). After the 1948 war, the tribe was expelled to Jordan (IDF 1954: 12-13). Abu-Khusa (1994: 83) tells us that after the 1948 war, the sheikh and his family (Abu-Sala'eh) were expelled to the Gaza Strip, while another part of the tribe was expelled to Jordan. In 1990, two leaders, *Mukhtars*, were appointed for two divisions of the tribe in Jordan: Hajj Yusef Mhammad Abu-Is'ayfan for the Abu-Is'ayfan tribe, and Hajj Harb Salem al-'Alaywat for the al-'Alaywat tribe.

Rawaw'a

The tribe's sheikh during the Mandate was Sallam 'Iyd Abu-Rawa', who was succeeded by Sheikh Hammad Msallam Abu-Rawa' (al-'Aref 1933: 47; 1934: 140-43). After the 1948 war, part of the tribe was expelled to Jordan with Sheikh Hammad Msallam Abu-Rawa' (IDF 1954: 12-13). Today the sheikh is Ahmad Hsein Mhammad Abu-Rawa'. Another part of the tribe, which was expelled to the Gaza Strip, is led by a *Mukhtar* Khalil 'Uthman Abu-Rawa' (Abu-Khusa 1994: 59- 60).

Sa'idiyin

In 1948 the population of the Sa'idiyin clan was estimated of 1,000 (IDF 1954: 13; Marx 1967: 11). According to al-Dabbagh (1991: 470), in 1931 its population was approximately 645.

Hamayitta

The tribe's sheikh during the Mandate was Suweilem 'Awda Ibn-Hamitta (al-'Aref 1933: 47; 1934: 154-59). After the 1948 war, the tribe was expelled to Jordan (Abu-Khusa 1994: 304-305; IDF 1954: 13).

Ramamneh

The tribe's sheikh during the Mandate was Suweilem 'Iyd Ibn-Raman (al-'Aref 1933: 47; 1934: 154-159), who was succeeded by his son, Sheikh Mhammad Suweilem Ibn-Raman. After the 1948 war, the sheikh and his tribe were expelled to Jordan (IDF 1954: 13).

Madhakir

The tribe's sheikh during the Mandate was 'Ali Naser Ibn-Dhekr (al-'Aref 1933: 47; 1934: 154-59). After the 1948 war, the sheikh and his tribe were expelled to Jordan (Abu-Khusa 1994: 304-305; IDF 1954: 13).

Rawayida

The tribe's sheikh during the Mandate was Salem Nassar Rawayidy (al-'Aref 1933: 47; 1934: 154-59), who was succeeded by his son, Sheikh Mhammad Salem Ibn- Rawayidy. After the 1948 war, the sheikh and his tribe were expelled to Jordan (Abu-Khusa 1994: 304-305; IDF 1954: 13). The Nkuz sub-tribe was also expelled to Jordan (IDF 1954: 13).

Swaiyat

After the 1948 war, Sheikh Sliman al-Swaiya and his tribe were expelled to Jordan (IDF 1954: 13).

Aheiwat

Most of the Aheiwat clan's land is in the Sinai, with some land and property in the southern part of Wadi 'Araba, in the vicinity of 'Aqaba. The name of the clan derives from a plant that flourishes in the Sinai in springtime; members of the clan were the first to eat its leaves and flowers (Launaea spp., *al-Huway*). The clan dispersed to different areas: the Sinai, 'Aqaba, Wadi 'Araba, and Southern Palestine. In 1931, the clan's population was approximately 420 (al-Dabbagh 1991: 474). In 1946, it was estimated to be 1,000 (IDF 1954: 14; Marx 1967:11). No mention is made of the clan having had a school before 1948.

Aheiwat control access to Sheikh Hmeid's tomb, which is on the Hejaz side of the Gulf of 'Aqaba. The tomb is visited by the Huweitat, Aheiwat, and al-'Imran tribes (al-'Aref 1944: 42-43; Stewart 1986: 1-44; Abu-Khusa 1994: 306-307; Shuqayr 1916: 117-20; Bailey 1980: 35-80; 1985: 21-49; Bailey and Peled 1975: 48-60).

According to Bar-Zvi, Abu-Rabi'a, and Kressel (1998: 103-4), approximately one kilometre from 'Ayn Ghadhyan is the tomb of saint al-Shuwahin, an object of pilgrimage and gathering site of the Aheiwat tribe. Such gatherings were known for their horse and camel races, in which Aheiwat men could demonstrate their prowess. According to Hajj Salameh Sbayyih Abu-Rabi'a (28 March 1983, personal communication) who had served in the area in Britain's camel-mounted forces (*al-Hajjaneh*) during the Mandate, al-Shuwahin was one of the founding fathers of the Aheiwat tribe.

During the Mandate, Aheiwat families would remain near the tomb for several days, pitch tents, and have the horse and camel races. Until 1948, members of the tribe in the Sinai would also participate.

Abu-Khalil

The tribe's sheikh during the Mandate was Mhammad Abu-Khalil. After the 1948 war, the sheikh and his tribe were expelled to Jordan (IDF 1994: 14).

Abu-Qadum

The tribe's sheikh during the Mandate was 'Iyd Abu-Qadum. After the 1948 war, the sheikh and his tribe were expelled to Jordan. The 'Atayqeh sub-tribe were also expelled to Jordan (IDF 1954: 14).

Jahalin

According to Marx (1967: 11) the population of the Jahalin clan was estimated at about 750 in 1948. The clan was expelled from its lands in Wadi Siyal, al-Hdaybeh, Mass'ada, al-Bqay'a, and Tall-Arad to the area of the Hebron Mountains (Abu-Khusa 1994: 310). Concerning the expulsion of the Jahalin clan, see Benny Morris (1996: 411, 531).

Abu-Dahuk

The tribe's sheikh during the Mandate was 'Abd al-'Aziz Nassar Abu-Dahuk, who came to power in 1930. He was succeeded by his son Sheikh Nassar in 1948, who in turn was succeeded by Sheikh 'Abd al-'Aziz Yusef Abu-Dahuk. The sheikh and his tribe were expelled to the Hebron Mountains after the 1948 war. Sheikh Isma'il Saqer Ibn Nassar Abu-Dahuk emigrated with part of his family to Jordan. In 1991, he served as a member of the Palestinian National Council (Abu-Khusa 1994:310).

Salamat al-Hersh

The tribe's sheikh during the Mandate was Rhayil al-Hersh, who was succeeded by Sheikh Ibrahim al-Hersh. The current sheikh is Mhammad Ibrahim al-Hersh (Abu-Khusa 1994: 310). There is another sub-tribe the al-Saray'eh, which also belongs to the Jahalin clan (Abu-Khusa 1994: 310).

Chapter 7

Bedouin Education in Arab Countries

*I*n order to know the educational problems that have faced and continue to face the Bedouin in Arab states, we must describe their social life, as well as economic, ecological and other parameters. According to Abu-Helal, Shammut, and Naser (1984) and Abu-Rabi'a (1994), the Bedouin in the Arab states can be classified by their patterns of living: nomadic, semi-nomadic, and settled Bedouin. In general, the traditional Bedouin are conservative people who maintain their ancestral rules, habits, and customs. The man is still the master of the house, and the women are completely dependent on the man for their living. They prefer boys to girls, educate boys rather than girls, and consider girls to be weak and suited only to working at home and looking after children. The Bedouin marry three or four wives, and teenage girls are often married to older men. The Bedouin see themselves as generous, courageous, brave, and charitable, yet take revengeful.

Studies of Bedouin social life, education, and settlements have explored some of their problems. Abd al-Dayim (1976: 57) describes how during the twentieth century, some of the Arab states have tried to settle the Bedouin, in order to solve their economic, social, and educational problems. Where settlement projects have succeeded, attendance of Bedouin children at schools has risen. According to Qubain (1966: 14), the problem of children in Bedouin nomadic tribes is likely to remain unresolved in the Arab states. Such children will probably be absorbed into the education system as most of the tribes gradually settle down. According to Szyliowicz (1973: 36), the nomadic Bedouin are an important group requiring integration into national life. While the spectacle of Bedouin riding their camels in the desert is still fairly common, it is becoming progressively less so. Modern advances in communications, transportation, and rural development have powerfully affected the Bedouin tribes. Furthermore, the perennial friction between the nomadic tribes and governments continues. The Bedouin comprise powerful autonomous groupings that freely wander over international borders, an intolerable state of affairs for any government. Middle Eastern governments have seized upon the challenge posed by this state of affairs to avail themselves of modern means of mobility and communications—jeeps, trucks, helicopters, radio—to extend their authority to remote and hitherto inaccessible areas dominated by the nomadic tribesmen.

According to Abu-Helal et al (1984), even the settled Bedouin encounter serious problems both social and economic in obtaining an education. Solving these problems requires strong, co-ordinated action by the responsible agencies of government. As of the 1980s, most Bedouin were illiterate. Fathers are anxious for their sons to study, and the sons are anxious to learn, yet when there is no chance to do so, they stop trying. Girls too are anxious to study, and realise how an education can help improve the conditions of their family's life. However, when faced with the obstructions they encounter, they lose hope. Both young men and women often have to discontinue their education to help their families earn a living.

According to Jabbur (1995: 391-420), among the camel-based Bedouin economies of the Middle East, educational institutions— even of the most elementary kind, which settled populations take for granted—are almost entirely unknown. Sheikhs of some of the larger tribes avail themselves of the services of a scribe (*kateb*) or religious spokesman (*khatib*) who has mastered the rudiments of literacy. This practice is most common amongst tribes in commercial contact with towns and villages, where they buy and sell livestock (mainly sheep) and enter into agreements with village people for tending livestock. Schools, either stationary or mobile, are virtually unknown in the desert. While the governments of most Arab countries have adopted provisions in their constitutions for the establishment of schools for the desert population, such provisions have generally remained dead letters. Over the years, various Arab governments have actually established mobile desert schools. However, they have not maintained them for long periods, and it is highly doubtful whether such schools have the potential for making a lasting impact in deep desert areas. They have, however, had some limited positive impact. When they were first established in desert border areas near villages, Bedouin boys would often satisfy their curiosity as to the trucks' destination the building materials they were carrying, and the building sites of schools. These boys sometimes went on to attend some classes, acquiring basic literacy and numeracy. They would usually lose interest quickly, though, and discontinue their attendance. Thus, the mobile schools did have some positive, albeit very short-term, impact. After all, while a school can be mobile, knowledge can be mobile only if its intended recipient is willing to learn.

Abu- Helal, Shammut, and Naser (1984: 57-67), report that when the Eastern Jordan Princedom (*Imaret sharq al-Urdon*) was established in 1921, there were 19 schools for boys with twenty seven teachers, and 2 schools for girls with two female teachers. The distribution of the 19 schools was as follows: 4 elementary schools (in Irbid, Karak, Ma'an, and al-Salt), and 15 literacy schools and *kuttab*. There were no secondary schools in Eastern Jordan. On the other hand, al-Maddy and Musa (1959: 309-11), report that there were 25 schools with fifty three male teachers and six female teachers. Most of the teachers came from Arab countries.

It should be noted that in 1922 the population of *Imaret sharq al-Urdon* was 225,380.

The Bedouin began to receive an education only after the establishment of the Bedouin forces (*Quwat al-Badiya*) in the Jordanian Army. They established guardposts (*makhafer*) for these forces in 1931, in such locations as, G-5, G-4, al-Jafr, and al-Azraq. These guardposts needed people who knew how to read and write, and use the wireless. Thus, the Army headquarters asked the teachers in the Ministry of Education to teach the guardpost personnel reading and writing. At that time the Jordanian Badiya was divided into the Northern Badiya, centred at al-Azraq, and the Southern Badiya, centred at al-Mudawwara (al-Jafr). In 1943 there were four schools at the following guardposts in the Badiya: G-4, al-Mafraq, al-Muwaqqar, and al-Azraq. These schools taught the soldiers how to read and write, and at the same time taught the sons of the tribes in that region.

The al-Risha area, in the Jordanian-Syrian Desert, is home to the Ruwala and Sha'lan tribes. Some of the tribes in the area have settled. The authorities established a primary school which had some seventy five pupils. The most significant aspect of this experience is settling the Bedouin and trying to integrate them into the mainstream of Jordanian society. When young Bedouin joined the army and security forces, their horizons expanded. These young Bedouin passed on what they had learnt to their tribal communities; this led other young Bedouin to join the Army. Thus different tribes were exposed to a new civilization and its rules. This new civilization was transmitted to the tribes by their own members, without being imposed by the authorities. Subsequently, the Army and security forces opened military schools especially for Bedouin children, where they studied, ate, and slept free of charge. When the children completed these military schools, they would join the Army. Educated Bedouin who lived in the towns would send their own children to school.

Some Bedouin in Jordan (Abu-Helal, Shammut, and Naser, 1984) live in the Badiya during the winter and spring, and become farmers during summer and autumn. The older generation go to the Badiya to take care of their livestock and cattle. The younger people live in villages, go to school, and take government and commercial jobs. The settling of the Bedouin in Jordan could be called natural development, without heavy expense, because it was part of the country's development programme. The authorities build villages and drill for deep ground water. The Bedouin live near village water resources and engage in agriculture. When the Bedouin settle in a village, the Ministry of Education opens schools.

According to Abu-Jaber and Gharaibeh (1981: 294-301), Jordan's urban expansion in areas close to traditional Bedouin territory has resulted in a considerable degree of voluntary urban settlement by the tribes. Sheikhs send their children to schools in the cities, and the government, for its part, has built schools and extended water and electrical supplies. Also, the Bedouin, as has been mentioned, have joined the military, and some scholarships have been arranged for Bedouin youth to study abroad. Furthermore, as the Bedouin have been absorbed into the urban economy, land prices have skyrocketed.

With education, the Bedouin have acquired the skills necessary for a modern economy, and many have left their tribes to take up outside employment, often sending part of their pay to their parents. Many less educated Bedouin have found employment in the military, where they have also undergone a process of institutionalisation. Some of the less educated have also found employment as hired farm laborers. Additional acculturation has been effected by the inauguration of social services as part of the resettlement programmes. All these factors have combined over the years to reduce the power of the sheikhs, who have been superseded to a certain extent by a new class of Bedouin leaders imbued with national awareness. Thus has transpired a process of weakening of tribal bonds.

In general, educated and professional people have refused to return to their tribes and to tend livestock. They move to permanent settlements where they find employment appropriate to their skills. Also, the employment of most of the tribes' men in the military has contributed to their abandonment of nomadism and their integration into urban Jordanian society.

According to Layne (1994: 43-46), the Jordanian government opened the first school for boys in the Jordan Valley in 1950. By 1981, in the rural Valley Deir 'Alla subdistrict alone, there were already twenty two elementary schools, nine each for boys and girls, and four mixed schools. Members of the 'Abbadis tribe mentioned the establishment of schools as a primary reason for their decision to give up a nomadic way of life. In fact, they made sure to settle in the vicinity of schools.

Education has had both economic and social impact on the Bedouin of the Jordan Valley. The very attendance of children at school reduced the number of shepherds. Also, men with some education soon began to marry outside their tribes, and in time, young women with schooling did so as well. The women went out of their way to take on citified, cultured airs, so as to attract educated men. Such young women also deemed it beneath their dignity to do traditional Bedouin women's chores, such as milking ewes and bringing flocks their fodder. Educated young Bedouin now have the skills required by the Jordanian economy's expanding service sector, many filling jobs created in the Jordan Valley area by the East Ghur Canal Project. Other educated young Bedouin commute to Amman and regional cities to fill government positions. As of 1980, however, there still were not enough educated people in the valley to fill all the job openings there; schools, hospitals and clinics, marketing centres, and the Jordan Valley Authority have all had to bringing people from other parts of the country, as well as non-Jordanian Arabs—Palestinians and people from other Arab countries—to fill positions.

Two examples of outside staffing of teaching positions are illustrative. As of 1980, all twelve teachers at the girls' secondary school at Deir 'Alla commuted from the regional capital, Salt. Of the twelve, only three had originally been Valley residents; one was from elsewhere in Jordan and five of the twelve were Palestinians. At the boys' secondary school at Mu'addi, out of twenty six teachers, only ten were originally from the Jordan Valley; eight were Palestinians, three Egyptians, and five from elsewhere in Jordan. Layne (1994: 90-91) noticed that a rise in the attendance of children at school in Jordan (where elementary schooling is now compulsory) has been accompanied by a decline in the contribution of children to agricultural productivity. This has been no less the case in the Jordan Valley region than elsewhere in the country. With Bedouin working outside the household economy, the range of economic tasks performed in the home is contracting, especially tasks traditionally performed by women. For example, as an increasing number of young women seek employment in offices and as teachers, mothers have become less inclined to teach their daughters traditional Bedouin methods of spinning and weaving. More and more food is obtained commercially nowadays, although girls still learn to brew special Bedouin coffee, bake Bedouin bread, and make yoghurt. As flock sizes continue to contract, less milk is processed into dairy products, and while older women still make butter and yoghurt, even they seldom make cheeses or drained yoghurt anymore. Furthermore, as crops have superseded livestock as the primary branch of agriculture, dairy processing has been replaced to a great extent by the processing of vegetables. It is also worth noting that expanded commercial performance of tasks once undertaken at home, mainly by women, has naturally been accompanied by altered loci of activity within the home, as well as altered use of household space that was formerly dedicated to storage.

Jabbur (1995: 282) also claims that successive Jordanian governments have managed to induce some Bedouin tribesmen to sedentise. He cites the example of Bani Sakhr tribesmen who have acquired agricultural land in desert borderlands and built permanent stone homes there. As of the 1960s, it was common for the sons of sheikhs to enroll in government schools and wear Western clothing.

Chatty (1990:133) also maintains that many Jordanian Bedouin are today undergoing a process of settlement in small rural communities. Furthermore, that process is succeeding, because planning is more sophisticated and, more importantly, because 'settled' life is becoming more attractive to the Bedouin themselves.

The petroleum-rich Gulf States (Abu-Helal, Shammut and Naser 1984) of Oman, Saudi Arabia, Kuwait, theUnited Arab Emirates, Qatar, Bahrain, and Iraq, have dealt with the Bedouin tribes by means other Arab states could not afford. Saudi Arabia, for example, has built agricultural settlements where the Bedouin continue to raise livestock and cattle. The authorities opened schools in these settlements. According to Cole (1975: 141-42), education is highly esteemed by the Bedouin. However, obtaining an education does not comport with the maintenance of a nomadic lifestyle. It is, in fact, in the field of education that the sedentary population has advanced the most, relative to the Bedouin. For example, among the al-Murrah in the period from 1968 to 1970, only three young men were enrolled in secondary schools in Saudi Arabia, and only one in Kuwait. Only a few dozen al-Murrah youngsters were enrolled in elementary school in the period under review. While secondary school attendance among the other tribes was somewhat better, Bedouin are a small minority in secondary schools, and almost no Bedouin was enrolled in university, either in Saudi Arabia or abroad. The Saudi Arabian educational effort has included the establishment of primary schools in villages and towns throughout the country, as well as the assignment of primary school teachers to accompany wandering tribes in the north, where large tribal groupings were concentrated. An increasing number of Bedouin children attend village schools, even though this entails separation from their families. It is unfortunate that village children taunt their Bedouin classmates for being poor and dirty. Studying the ecology of Bedouin elementary school in the Hail Province of Saudi Arabia, al-Eisa (1985), found that Bedouin children felt they were inferior and even town-children made fun of them. In the al-Murrah tribe, boys of families staying in the Hofuf and Abquaiq areas attended village schools for only a few years, until they have mastered basic reading, writing, and arithmetic.

Given the value the Bedouin attach to education, stressing the greater availability of educational services is a major part of the government's sedentisation campaign among the nomadic tribes.

Among the proposals for making education more available to
Bedouin children is the establishment of schools in oases where the
tribes often camp in the summer. Such a project could be conducted
at Jabrin, for example. The school at Jabrin remains open during
the fall, winter, and spring, with only a handful of students. It closes
in June for the summer holidays, just when the mass of the al-Jaber
clan arrives at the oasis for three months, during which neither
children nor adults have very much to do. Yet another proposal
would involve making dormitories available to young Bedouin interested in post-primary schooling in the towns. In the 1970 school
year, for instance, six al-Murrah boys aged twelve to sixteen lived
alone in Haradh in tin and scrap lumber shacks, doing all their
own cooking and housework, in order to attend the middle school
there. Had more facilities been available, many more boys would
gladly have attended. Instruction in fields of particular use to the
Bedouin economy, such as livestock and range management, integrated into the general school curriculum, would be eagerly sought
by many bright Bedouin youngsters. Yet many Bedouin find it difficult to adjust in schools designed mainly for the sedentary population. Thus, many bright young Bedouin who have the potential to
be successful in the modern economy are condemned to employment as unskilled and semi-skilled labourers, or in the military, for
lack of educational qualifications.

In one Bedouin settlement studied in Wadi Fatima, Saudi Arabia
(Katakura 1977: 62-65), the social development centre was charged
with raising local social, cultural, agricultural, educational, and public health and hygiene standards. For instance, the centre finances
tuition-free elementary schools, mainly in the homes of teachers;
such schools are attended by some 80 per cent of the children in the
area. The Saudi government pays teachers' salaries and also pays for
children's textbooks, writing materials, and schoolbags. Parents
tend to be enthusiastic about education, as they see it as a means for
their children's advancement. The enrolment of one child in school
often has a snowball effect: the parents of other children also
become interested. During peak agricultural seasons, however, children usually remain at home to help with work. Children tend to be
serious about their studies, as well as competitive- final examination
grades are posted in the newspapers. There is the story of one Wadi
Fatima boy who finished first in his class: relatives came from all
over the country for a banquet his parents gave in his honour, at

which he made a speech. Despite the enthusiasm for education, though, fewer than 10 per cent of Wadi Fatima elementary school graduates go on to secondary school, which requires boarding at Mecca or Jedda. Most students who do continue study at technical schools, with the aim of qualifying in business or engineering. When parents get together and decide they want a school, they inform the Ministry of Education, which finances a teacher through the social development centre. Often, other basic school requirements, such as a portable blackboard and chalk, are provided. There are no desks or chairs at a school; Bedouin children sit on their knees and write, as did their forebears, on their knees on a cloth or palm-leaf mat on the sand. News of the opening of a new school is advertised in the newspapers, and then spreads by word of mouth.

On the border between the United Arab Emirates and Oman, south-west of al-'Ayn at al-Wajan (Abu-Helal, Shammut, and Naser 1984), there is a huge concentration of Bedouin settlements: al-'Awamir, al-Manahil, al-Manassir, al-Duru', 'Afar, al-Shawamis, and al-Hududiya. These tribes raise camels and other livestock, and move back and forth across the border. There are elementary and (coeducational) junior high schools, and there is a military school, from the third grade, for the Bedouin boys. The Bedouin prefer such schools, because the boys are paid salaries, and receive uniforms and other benefits which are dispensed to entice the Bedouin to to get an education.

In Oman, according to Mohammed (1981:336), the government has ambitious plans for Bedouin areas, especially in the five-year plan for 1981-85. Chiefly involved are schemes for health, education, social services, housing, veterinary services, and water supply.

Kuwait (Abu- Helal, Shammut and Naser 1984) builds special houses for Bedouin who want to settle in the cities. The Bedouin often are enthusiastic about being settled. In each settlement, they open a handsome school structure. The same pattern prevails in the United Arab Emirates, Qatar, and Bahrain. According to al-Musallam (1984), female students at secondary school in Kuwait have high aspirations for further education and gainful employment as they are willing to postpone marriage in order to enable them to exercise their options. However, the students view child rearing and homemaking as the primary tasks of women.

Jabbur (1995: 283), tells of meeting Sheikh 'Ajil al-Yawir, one of the noted sheikhs of Iraq's Shammar tribe, in the early years of the twentieth century, at the home of the president of the American University in Beirut. Jabbur, who was impressed by the extent of Sheikh al-Yawir's knowledge of world affairs, subsequently lectured at the American University to a class attended by the sheikh's son, Sheikh Sfuq, before the latter assumed the reigns of tribal leadership.

In Iraq (Abu-Helal, Shammut, and Naser 1984), the settlement of the Bedouin was largely motivated by the desire to spread literacy amongst them. The towns of Nasiriyyah and Ramadi were established by Midhat Pasha in 1869 and 1870, mainly as centres for the Bedouin population (Gerber 1985: 238; Longrigg 1925: 298-324). Appointed Wali of Baghdad in 1869, Midhat Pasha dealt with the tribal issue through the institution of land grants. He proved to be the greatest Ottoman governor ever assigned to Iraq. He believed that once the Bedouin altered their nomadic lifestyle and were tied to the soil, they would become dependent on the government.

Even before Midhat Pasha, the Bedouin had very gradually begun to settle. Yet the Ottoman administration had, by oppressions and injustices committed by its officials, actually discouraged Bedouin settlement. From the outset, many nomadic tribes were aware of the actual aims of the Ottoman policy of sedentisation, or at least suspected those aims, and did not avail themselves of the land grant privilege. Some tribes that had so availed themselves often reverted to nomadism, after being subjected to abuses by government officials. In some cases, part of a tribe would embrace a settled lifestyle and engage in agriculture, while the other part would preserve the nomadism of its forefathers.

Among the more salient examples of Bedouin that settled and took up agriculture is the Muntafiq clan in the central Euphrates region, along with several tribes that dwelt along the Tigris. It would be fair to say that the Ottoman administration had not made a serious attempt to engender conditions conducive to the settlement of nomadic tribes, or to their advancement, either materially or socially. Actually, the opposite may have been the case: tribes close to settled areas tended to engage more in bloodshed and predation than those that dwelt in the desert. The Sa'dun tribe of the Muntafiq clan on the Euphrates serves as an illustrative example of the forces unleashed by the new policy of settlement. Nasir of the Sa'dun was appointed Pasha by Midhat, with the aim of bringing the Muntafiq to heel. He became a willing tool of the Ottoman administration, accepting high office under the Porte authorities, and founded the city of Nasiriyyah. On the other hand, his brother Mansur led the faction in the tribe that was hostile to innovation. Another example is that of the Shammar Jarba tribe. When Farhan Ibn-Sufuk was appointed Pasha, with the understanding that he would help to settle his nomadic tribe, he visited Istanbul, married town-bred women, gave his sons a Turkish education, and farmed his lands at Sharqat on the Tigris. His tribesmen were offended by all this, and by the Turkish airs he affected, with the result that one faction of the tribe, under Faris, seceded and maintained the free, nomadic lifestyle of its forefathers.

One particularly noticeable effect of the twin Ottoman policy of settlement and Ottomanisation was the undermining of the tribal spirit. This, in fact, was the policy of both the Iraqi pashas and the Porte in Istanbul. As applied to the Kurds, it was mainly intended assure their loyalty to the Khalifate by means of salaried positions; there had never been any intention as such of having the Kurds forgo tribalism (Jamali 1934: 56-57; Longrigg 1925: 306-9). During the rule of Midhat Pasha (Shamir 1965: 249-52), many Bedouin took it upon themselves to cease opposing the government, to take up permanent domicile, build homes, regularly pay their taxes, and not to neglect cultivation of the land.

The establishment of Nasiriyya, with its public services and institutions, was truly a noteworthy accomplishment. The city was planned with the aid of a Belgian engineer, and was intended to be the regional capital of the Muntafiq. A member of the Sa'dun family of Muntafiq was appointed as the *mutasarrif*, and included in the Ottoman provincial hierarchy. However, Midhat's main accomplishment, settlement of the Bedouin on the land, actually yielded negative results. Most of the land alienated to small cultivators ended up in the hands of urban notables or assertive tribal heads. The settlement of Bedouin tribes did have partial success, in that it reduced the pressures of tribal aggression and involved many Bedouin in agricultural production. In the final analysis, Midhat's enterprise failed because it was a single endeavour for which the times were not yet ripe. Midhat was greeted with feelings ranging from suspicion to enmity, with both Bedouin and town dwellers rejecting his innovations and refusing to co-operate with him. Finally, his superiors in Istanbul pulled the rug out from underneath him.

The circumstances of Algeria, with its large area and bitter colonial legacy, are unique. The Algerian authorities have conducted a survey of pastoral areas, and opened a school in a central location, where tribes gather. The nomads' schools, *al-Madares al-Ra'awiya*, are dedicated to teaching Badiya children. In general, due to its unique situation, Algeria has been moving slowly in regard to Bedouin education (Abu-Helal, Shammut and Naser 1984).

In southern Sudan, according to Khogali (1981: 302-17), some of the nomads have found occupations in farming, trade, driving, work in markets, and maintenance and repairs, in permanent settlements. Some nomads have acquired an education and become teachers; such people generally do not return to their tribes, preferring the permanent settlements. Better educational and economic opportunities are generally the reasons for remaining in permanent settlements. Khogali found that children from the age of eight take care of the flock, while women help when the flock is in the vicinity of the tents. As the children get older, they take care of larger flocks, and by the time they are adults they are able to care for a herd of camels. A similar situation exists among Bedouin tribes in Cyrenaica of Lybia (Evans-Pritchard 1949), among the Ruwala tribes in Jordan, and in the Arabian Peninsula (Lancaster 1981).

Mohammed (1973) analyses the cotton programme of the White Nile in Sudan, where nomads and dwellers in permanent housing complement each other. Families of those Bedouin who remain shepherds live on the agricultural farms during the cotton-harvesting season and work for local families. When a hired labourer becomes a shepherd, his family generally continues to maintain social relations with the family of his former employer.

Among the Bedouin in the Western Desert of Egypt, Ismael (1976:153) found that some of the boys went to school, but most of them worked with the flocks. The girls collected firewood, brought water from the cisterns, and helped their mothers in running the home.

According to Karni (1976), nineteen schools were in operation in the southern Sinai, attended by some 400 Bedouin children. Until 1967, only three schools had been in operation in the region: al-Tur, Abu Znima, and Wadi Firan. The schools at al-Tur and Abu Znima were for the children of Egyptian labourers. Most of the pupils were boys. In several of the schools, there were no girls at all. The overall proportion of girls in the schools was some 5 per cent. Most schools had an enrolment of 15-30 pupils, who typically commenced their studies at age eleven or twelve. Most of the schools comprised a master class, which was divided into various study levels. The teacher instructed the children of the various levels concurrently. The schools of the southern Sinai employed 23 teachers, 20 of whom were local Bedouin, while three were brought to the region from al-'Arish. The main subjects of instruction were reading and writing (in Arabic), arithmetic, and religion. Other subjects were taught as well. The children received one free hot meal every day, which included legumes, pita bread, and tea. The food was prepared by a school employee. The introduction of free meals considerably helped to raise school attendance. According to Zbida (1975), copybooks, pens, and pencils were also distributed free to the pupils.

The need to help with the family's work or find outside employment was one of the main reasons that boys did not attend school. Likewise, the raising of livestock, mainly a distaff chore, was one of the main reasons more girls did not attend school. The first girls to attend school were the daughters of sheikhs, of Egyptian labourers, and of school teachers. After one girl had enrolled, the number of girls would tend to steadily rise over time, as if the path had been cleared (Karni, 1976).

The impact of tribal migration on regular school attendance tends to vary from one locality of the southern Sinai to another. The people of Dahab, to give one example, organised school transportation during the migration season. The Ramsa school, owned by the Hamadah, Sawalha, and 'Ulayqat tribes, was transferred to a tent that follows the tribes in the migration season. The fact that the teacher was a Hamadah facilitated the school's mobility. Nevertheless, migration did affect attendance at Bedouin schools. Sometimes migration caused a seasonal decline in attendance approaching 50 per cent (Karni 1976). According to Zbida (1975), there was a high drop-out rate among schoolchildren in the southern Sinai for a variety of reasons, the most important of which was the migration of parents. Sometimes pupils would leave school for several months, and then return to resume their studies from where they had left off. On the other hand, children would sometimes commence their studies in the middle of a school year.

In the view of Karni (1976) and Zbida (1975), a request by a sheikh for a school is usually the main impetus for inducing the authorities to establish a school. The establishment of a school is tangible evidence of the respect the authorities have for a sheikh. A school tends to enhance a sheikh's standing with his tribe, and his tribe's standing with other tribes. Furthermore, sheikhs want supportive power behind them—the power of advisors who know how to read and write. Literacy and numeracy are prerequisites for economic advancement, and often for obtaining outside employment. Proficiency in reading and writing is also necessary for dealing with the authorities, providers of medical services, and outside traders, among others. Education is perceived as an important tool for understanding the outside world. Even the most rudimentary education has become a status symbol. The very act of studying has become a source of honour and pride. Furthermore, the school has become increasingly perceived as a natural place for children to be, even though education is not compulsory in the southern Sinai.

It should be noted that in some tribes in the Western Desert of Egypt, a peripatetic teacher used to wander with the tribe and teach the tribe's sons (Cole and Altorki 1998: 77; Kennet 1968: 146-47). In the 1960s, Bedouin youth began to get primary education from school teachers sent by the state to the new settlements in their area. Some of the Bedouin school children walked for a couple of hours or more to get to school (Cole and Altorki 1998: 99, 102). Education led to highly paid and respectable jobs. In the late 1970s, there were about three hundred young men from Marsa Matruh in Egyptian universities; about 50 per cent of them were Bedouin students (Abou-Zeid 1979: 283-90). In the Marsa Matruh governorship, about 58 per cent of the population over ten years old was illiterate in 1968 and about 22 per cent could read and write only. However, there were 1,411 people with university degrees and six with post graduate degrees (Cole and Altorki 1998: 12).

The Bedouin tribes of the Beqa'a Valley (Chatty 1978: 399-415), including al-Fadl and al-Hassanna, are mainly engaged in raising sheep and goats. The Beqa'a Valley, politically part of Lebanon, is a natural continuation of the plain of Homs in Syria; the Bedouin tribes in the area migrate around the region of the Lebanon-Syria border. All members of nomadic families engaged in traditional husbandry lend a hand in the work. Such tasks as tending young and sick animals, milking (goats, sheeps, and camels), and churning surplus milk into butter and selling it to middlemen have traditionally been entrusted to the women. Furthermore, it is the women who dismantle the tents when a move must be made to better grazing areas, and reassemble them at their destination. The men in Bedouin households are charged with herding livestock, shearing wool, and dealing with local farmers and landowners with whom they enter into grazing and camel service arrangements. Ordinarily, during periods of peak agricultural activity, an elderly household member, either man or woman, takes care of the young children. Until relatively recent times, two or three boys would ordinarily be engaged in tending the sheep and goats, which would be taken to pasture in areas adjacent to dwelling areas. At the same time, at least two strong men would handle the camels, which would be used for hauling harvests. When trucks came into use, there was less of a need to pull up camp to follow optimal grazing; sheep now graze as far as ten miles from dwelling areas. As a result, small boys no longer work as shepherds; it is a task now assigned to the older boys in a household, and to hired men.

Single women have traditionally helped married women in their work. Nowadays, however, with a reduction in the frequency of camp relocations, young women do seasonal work in nearby areas. As tribes came to migrate less and became more permanent in particular areas, they began to enter into longer-term labour agreements with farmers and large landowners. In the earlier periods, such contracts would be for the labour of the older boys. By the early 1970s, however, agreements were already being concluded for groups of young women in the fields; their employers would collect them in the morning and bring them back to their encampments after work. Hence, greater residential permanency has led to a reduction in requirements for female labour by the tribes, releasing young people for gainful outside employment. Beginning in their late teens, young men do seasonal work on the farms, setting aside some of their income for future marriage expenses. Young women typically work from sunrise to mid-afternoon in the fields. After returning home, they help with various household tasks, such as looking after younger brothers and sisters, washing, sweeping, and fetching well water.

Chatty (1990:128) reports that among Syrian Bedouin tribes such as the Fed'aan, al-Hassanna, and al-Fadl the adoption of the truck as a means of transportation over the last ten or fifteen years has expanded their traditional economic sphere, and opened new economic horizons. These tribes, with the mobility trucks afford, have been able to develop a viable and highly profitable economic system which integrates pastoralism with agriculture. A similar situation has developed over the past ten years among the Jordanian and Saudi Arabian Bedouin tribes, whose half-ton trucks are now a common sight at encampments.

According to Bahhady (1981: 258-66), the first co-operative for the nomadic herdsmen on the Syrian plain was established in 1968. The co-operatives provide the herdsmen with such essential services as credit facilities, health care, veterinary surgeons, and storage facilities for their livestock feed. Furthermore, they provide whatever educational facilities are available to the nomads. At present, the literacy rate amongst the plains Bedouin is roughly 10 per cent. Various ideas concerning ways this rate can be raised have been mooted, among them the operation of community-based, tuition-free boarding schools during the peak migration period, which lasts from October to late February.

The importance of properly planning social policies aimed at changing the Bedouin lifestyle cannot be over-emphasised, and neither can the proper implementation of such policies, through pedagogical effort and extension campaigns. Bedouin parents are often extremely enthusiastic about the prospects of sending their children to school. In some communities, a local man will assume the role of teacher, instructing the young in the Quran in one of the local residences. Parents have shown themselves willing to have their children study three to four months a year, and to pay for the instruction. The 'Aniza and other Bedouin tribes in Syria (Lewis 1987: 71) were also affected by the extension of cultivation and of government authority. Like Jad'an of the Fid'an and other 'Aniza sheikhs, Sheikh Farhan ibn Hudayb, sheikh of the Sba'ah 'Abdah, adapted to the new conditions and turned them to his own advantage, acquiring land and employing farmers to cultivate it. In 1892 his son, Barjas, was sent by order of the government to the tribal school Asiret Mektebi for the sons of sheikhs in Istanbul. Barjas served as an officer in the army before returning to Syria to succeed his father in 1906. Other young Syrian sheikhs, among them Nawaf as-Salih, the future sheikh of the Hadidiyin, also studied at Istanbul. Faysal Ibn-Husayn, future King of Syria and then of Iraq, was another student at the Asiret Mektebi.

According to Jabbur (1995: 391-20), sometimes Bedouin sheikhs who sit in the national legislature and have seen for themselves the benefits of education will have several of their sons accompany them to the city while the legislature is in session, so they can go to school. Also, some sheikhs have married city women and spend part of their time in the cities, where they send their sons to school. Then there are those sheikhs who have simply come to recognise the importance of learning. Oft-times such men have sent for teachers from the outside to accompany their encampments and teach their sons. These three types of cases, however, involve only a tiny minority of Bedouin; they cannot serve as a basis for drawing general conclusions. Most of the knowledge Bedouin boys have traditionally received come from the tribal social gathering (*majles*), where they listen to stories of their tribe's history, wars, and folklore, as well as to Arabic poetry, and general world events. Nevertheless, three examples of sheikhs who have valued learning can shed some useful light on the phenomenon.

One is the late Sheikh Trad Ibn-Milhim, of the Hsana tribe in the region of Hims. He was a self-educated man, who spent much of his time reading newspapers. When Jabbur was invited to his majles in the 1950s, he felt himself in the presence of a man who much esteemed learning. Another self-educated sheikh was Amir Nayif el-Sha'lan, of the Ruwala, in the Syrian desert. A man who avidly read newspapers, magazines, and books, Amir Nayif sat in the Syrian parliament, where he was the leader of a block of tribal deputies much courted by the powers that be for its pivotal influence. In his private affairs, Amir Nayif applied advanced agricultural techniques to his farm in Jabal al-Barida. His two daughters by one of his wives, a relative he married, studied in Damascus and mastered foreign languages. Amir Nayif's nephew, Amir Mut'ib, also a deputy in the national legislature and son of the paramount Ruwala sheikh, Amir Fawwaz, provides another example. Amir Mut'ib, who is fluent in English, studied at several of Syria's schools and under tutors who accompanied his tribe in the desert.

Abu-Rabi'a (1994a: 61) found that among the Negev Bedouin in the 1980s, various situations determined whether the woman and her daughters fed the flock: they did so when the husband and younger brothers were away from home, doing outside work, or studying; when there were several girls in the house, more than the number required for the housework; and when the flock was owned by a widow who could not afford to hire a shepherd, or who wanted to save expenses. Children every where contributed to the livestock economy, some of them before and after attending school during the day, every day of the week. On weekends, on Fridays,

and during the school holidays, both adults and children participated in the work with the flock more than on ordinary days. Since
the care of the flock requires many working hands almost round the
clock, all members of the family work at it. This made it difficult for
the pupils to prepare their school homework properly, and had an
adverse effect on their progress in their studies. Because of the top
priority given by most families to their livestock, it was difficult for
some of the children to start school at an early age. They often gave
up their studies to care for the flock. Identification with the flock
was stronger than the urge to acquire an education, although many
families do regard an education as an economic asset, a powerful
resource which should be developed and exploited. Marx (1967:
83) found that among the Negev Bedouin in the 1960s, small flocks
were taken to pasture by children of the owners. In the 1920s and
1930s, al-'Aref (1933: 170) found that shepherding among the
Negev Bedouin was the work of children of both sexes; he never
saw a man or woman do it.

Problems facing Bedouin Education in Arab States

Some of the problems that the Bedouin must confront in the pursuit
of education (Abu-Helal, Shammut, and Naser 1984; Abu-Rabi'a
1994; Mahjub 1981) are detailed below.

1. *Scarcity of schools in the desert:* The research team never
   saw a school in Jordan's Arabian Desert, nor in the deserts
   of the other states it visited. The desert is a natural
   obstruction to aid to the Bedouin, who constantly move
   from place to place in search of water and pasture land for
   their livestock. They change camp three or four times a
   year, moving up to forty kilometres each time.
2. *Shortage of schools:* All settlements and encampments
   suffer from a school shortage. There are simply not
   enough places for all children of school age. In the
   majority of these settlements, there is co-education in
   elementary and preparatory classes.
3. *Poor Quality of education:* The quality of education is
   poor, and this is so mainly for the two reasons already
   mentioned: the scarcity of schools, and the fact that most

desert schools function only at the elementary level. Thus, a pupil who wishes to continue on to a secondary education may not find any facilities at a reasonable distance from where he lives. The solution, to board near a school, is usually too costly.

4. *Location of schools for Bedouin:* Schools are far from where Bedouin live. Roads are generally poor, and sometimes do not even exist between residential areas and the schools. Where roads do exist, there is often no transportation. This causes financial and social problems for Bedouin who want to send their children to school. During a field visit which the research team conducted in Jordan's Saudi desert, the team met a ten-year-old boy at al-Muwaqqar village, walking to school on foot in a poor road. They asked him why he was going to school on foot. He said no transportation was available. They then asked him if he went to school alone or with other pupils. He answered that he went with two other children, but they were absent that day. He told them he walked to school all year round, suffering from cold in winter and heat in summer. He said no cars passed along the route to school, only some trucks or water containers, and not regularly; when they did, through, the drivers gave them a lift. The team realised from this incident that transportation is a severe problem for Bedouin school children, and if the school is too far for example, ten kilometers away children simply do not go to school.

5. *Financial problems:* The Bedouin are generally poor, and if a school is far from their settlements, they have to rent homes near the school in a village, where their children can stay. The need to pay for all the expenses of a child living away from home is usually a very heavy burden on Bedouin parents. Those Bedouin who finish school often feel they have enough education already and then obtain low-paying employment. Some of them became soldiers or find other jobs.

6. *Social problems resulting from distance:* Renting accomodations near a school forces the mother of the schoolchild to stay with him, thus splitting the family; the father stays home, with his other wives, to look after the

livestock. If the mother cannot stay with her child at
school, an elder sister is sent. The research team came
across such split families in Jordan's Arabian Desert.

7. *Psychological problems resulting from distant schools:* As
   the Bedouin child must walk a long distance to school,
   suffering from cold in winter and the heat in summer, he
   often asks himself what the advantage of education is if he
   has to tend sheep after he finishes school. As the Bedouin
   child returns home from school very tired, and still has to
   help his family to look after livestock, he has no time to do
   his homework. The research team came to realise that
   education in Bedouin settlements has a very low priority
   compared to education in cities. Thus Bedouin prefer to
   acquire an elementary education and then go to military
   school or join the National Guard, in Arab countries.

8. *Social situation of Bedouin and education:* Bedouin live
   in clans that comprise tribes, which in turn comprise
   extended families. Each tribe is ruled by a sheikh, and has
   its own rules and customs. The research team believes that
   Bedouin see education as a means of changing their
   economic, but not social, circumstances. Yet the majority
   of Bedouin who live in settlements do not send their sons
   to school-they want their sons to work. The research team
   also interviewed school age girls who left school. They had
   done so to free their mothers to help their fathers tend the
   livestock. The team also met girls who had never gone to
   school, for the same reason.

9. *Bedouin economic circumstances and education:* We have
   already seen that the Bedouin family is an integrated
   economic unit. Everyone has a job: the man and his wife
   tend to the livestock, the girls do housework, the sons help
   their fathers do strenuous tasks, such as bring livestock to
   market. The work is hard and lasts from morning till
   evening. Thus, having children in school means fewer
   working hands, lending to a lower family income.
   Furthermore, as desert schools are far from most
   settlements, sending a child to school entails rental of a
   home, and this is an expense few Bedouin are willing to
   shoulder.

The Transformation of Bedouin Life:

Most Arab governments have furthered the sedentisation of the nomadic Bedouin. In fact, some Arab governments have made this an important objective, although such policies have had limited impact in the deep desert areas as most Bedouin have continued to cling to their traditional ways. Yet even in desert areas there has been change. Tribes have eagerly adopted the automobile as the principal means of transport, after circumstances forced them to change their main economic branch from camel to sheep breeding. On another plane, Bedouin tribes no longer appeal to arms and violence in disputes amongst themselves; agreements between sheikhs and the laws adopted by Arab states have brought such instances of internecine effusion of blood to an end in the modern world. Furthermore, with many young Bedouin joining the military, their habits of work, diet, and dress undergo thorough change. They have then gone on to bring up their own children in the new ways, which become further entrenched, as the young generation attend schools in the towns.

The sedentisation programmes of Arab governments (Jabbur, 1995: 525-37) have included the building of schools and medical clinics. The Bedouin have acquired faith in Western medicine, and show every inclination to avail themselves of hospitals and modern medicine. In fact, the Bedouin have become fairly health conscious. Changed lifestyles are further reflected in ways of earning a living. The women in some Bedouin villages pick cotton for wealthy villagers in the cotton season. Also, many Bedouin have found employment with the oil companies, especially Aramco. The constitutions of most Arab states now contain provisions for Bedouin education. Certain fairly simple programmes, such as mobile schools or teachers who travel with the nomadic Bedouin, have been adopted to help disseminate literacy. In the upper stratum of the Bedouin, the sons of sheikhs now sometimes attend school in towns, where they adopt the urban mode of dress while retaining the traditional Bedouin *Kufiya* and *'iqal* headdress. For example, Jabbur relates visiting Sheikh Haditha, all of whose sons were studying in government schools in Amman. The boys all wore Western dress. He also relates that when at university, he had tutored a Bedouin student named Farhan Shbaylat, who went on to become an overseas ambassador for Jordan. In his school days, he became Western in his ways, as have many young Jordanian Bedouin.

Suggestions for the Bedouin in the Middle East

1. Prepare the financial framework required for spending on education.
2. Establish of the necessary organisational and staff infrastructure in each Arab state to advance education amongst the Bedouin tribes.
3. Examine the exact nature, numbers, and conditions of the Bedouin refugees in the Gaza Strip, the West Bank, Jordan, and Sinai.
4. Find out how many Bedouin refugees would want to return to their home lands in the Negev.
5. Investigate the role the UN, USA, European countries, Israel, and Arab countries might play in solving the problems of Bedouin refugees in the Middle East.

References

Abcarius, Michael F. 1946. *Palestine Through the Fog of Propoganda*. London: Hutchinson and Co.

Abd al-Dayim, Abdallah. 1976. *al-Tarbiya fi al-Bilad al-'Arabiya*. Beirut: Dar al-'Ilm lil-Malayin.

Abd al-Kader [Qadir], Qasem. 1978. Education among the Bedouin Population in the Negev. *Hachinuch, Educational Psychology Review*.51, no. 1: 94-95.

Abou-Zeid, Ahmad. 1979. New Towns and Rural Development in Egypt. *Africa* 49, no. 3: 283-90.

Abu Helal, Ahmad, Usama Shammut, and Ibrahim Naser. 1984. *Taisir Ta'lim al-Badw fi al-watan al-'Arabi*. Tunis: Idarat al-Buhuth al-Tarbawiya, al-Munazzama al-'Arabiya li-Tarbiya wal-Thaqafa wal-'Ulum.

Abu-Jaber, Kamel, and Fawzi Gharaibeh. 1981. Bedouin Settlement, Organizational, Legal and Administration Structure in Jordan. *The Future of Pastoral Peoples*, edited by J. G. Galaty et al., Ottawa: The International Development Centre.

Abu-Khusa, Ahmad. 1976-1979. *Beer al-Saba' wal-hayah al-Badawiya* (in Arabic). Amman: Matabi' al-Mu'assasa al-Sahafiya al-Urdunniya.

_____. 1994. *Mausw'at Qabayil Beer al-Saba' wa-'Ashairiha al-Raiysiah* (in Arabic). Amman: Sherket al-Sharq al-Awsat le-Teba'a.

Abu-Mu'eileq, Tawfiq. 1990: *al-Naqab wal-Qaba'el al-Badawiya fi Filastin* (in Arabic). Demashq: Matba'at Ibn-Khaldun.

Abu-Rabi'a, 'Aref. 1983. Folk Medicine among the Bedouin Tribes in the Negev. Sde Boqer: Social Studies Center at Blaustein Institute for Desert Research.

_____.1993. Educational Anthropology in Bedouin Society. *Practicing Anthropology*15, no.2: 21-23.

_____ 1994a. *The Negev Bedouin and Livestock Rearing: Social, Economic and Political Aspects*. Oxford: Berg.

_____ 1994b. The Bedouin Refugees in the Negev. *Refuge*14, no. 6:15-17.

_____ 1997. *Dropping out in Bedouin Schools*. Research Report to the Ministry of Education. Beersheba: Ministry of Education.

_____ 1999a. Veterinary and Medicinal Plants among Bedouin Tribes. *Herbs, Humans and Animals*. Koln: Experiences Verlag.

_____ 1999b. Some Notes on Livestock Production among Negev Bedouin Tribes. *Nomadic Peoples*3, no.1: 22-30.

Abu-Rabi'a, Aref, and Dov Barnea 1998. *Statistical Data about Bedouin Schools*. Research Report to the Ministry of Education. Beersheba: Ministry of Education.

Abu-Saad, Ismael.1991. Towards an Understanding of Minority Education in Israel: the Case of the Bedouin Arabs of the Negev. *Comparative Education* 27, no. 2: 235-42.

_____ 1988. Minority Higher Education in an Ethnic Periphery: The Bedouin Arabs. *Ethnic Frontiers and Peripheries, Landscape of Development and Inequality in Israel*, edited by O. Yiftachel and A. Meir. Boulder, Colorado: Westview Press.

Abu-Sitta: *Ma'in Abu-Sitta Society*. 1994.

Abu-Sitta, Salman. 1995. *Al-'Arab al-Mansiyun: Badw Beer al-Saba'*. Parts 1 and 2. *Alhayat*, no.11906: 27; no. 11907: 28.

Afinish, al-, Selim. 1987. Processes of Change and Continuity in a Kinship System and Family Ideology in Bedouin Society. *Sociologia Ruralis* 27: 323-340.

Akarli, Engid. 1986. Abdulhamid II's Attempt to Integrate Arabs into the Ottoman System. *Palestine in the late Ottoman Period:Political, Social and Economic Transformation*, edited by David Kushner. Leiden and Jerusalem: E. J. Brill and Yad Izhak Ben-Zvi.

Alsberg, Paul. 1975. The Israel State Archives as a Source for the History of Palestine During the Period of Ottoman Rule. *Studies on Palestine During the Ottoman Period*, edited by M. Ma'oz. Jerusalem: The Magnes Press of The Hebrew University, Institute of Asian and African Studies, and Yad Izhak Ben-Zvi.

Anglo-American Committee for inquiry. 1946. *A Survey of Palestine*. Table 8b.

al- 'Aref, 'Aref. 1933. *Al-Qada bayna al-Badw*. Jerusalem: Bayt al-Maqdes.

_____ 1934. *Tarikh Beer al-Saba' wa-Qabai'liha*. Jerusalem: n.p.

_____ 1944. *Bedouin Love, Lore and Legend*. Jerusalem: Cosmo.

_____ 1973. 'Aref al-'Aref papers (in Arabic) no.8. Beirut: Markez al-Abhath al-Filastiniya. PLO.

Asad, Talal. 1970. *The Kababish Arabs: Power, Authority, and Consent in a Nomadic Tribe*. London: Hurst and Company.

Aurel, Alexander and Peretz Cornfeld. 1945. *The Near And Middle East: WHO'S WHO*. Vol. 1, Palestine, Trans-Jordan 1945-1946.

Jerusalem: The Near East and Middle East WHO'S WHO Publishing Company.

Avitsur, Shmuel. 1976. *Daily Life in Eretz Israel in the Nineteenth Century* (in Hebrew). Jerusalem: 'Am Hasefer.

Bahhady, Faik, A. 1981. Recent Changes in Bedouin Systems of Livestock Production in the Syrian Steppe. *The Future of Pastoral People*, edited by J. G. Galaty et al. Ottawa: The International Development Centre.

Bailey, Clinton. 1980. The Negev in the Nineteenth Century: Reconstructing History from Oral Traditions. *Asian and African Studies* 14: 35-80.

_____. 1981. Notes on the Bedouin Population of the Gaza Strip. *Notes on the Bedouins*, no.12: 45-53.

_____.1982. Bedouin War Poems from the Negev. *Studies in Arabic and Islam* 3: 131-164.

_____. 1985. Dating the Arival of the Bedouin Tribes in Sinai and the Negev. *Journal of the Economic and Social History of the Orient* 28: 20-49.

_____. 1991. *Bedouin Poetry, from Sinai and the Negev*. Oxford: Clarendon Press.

_____. 1989. The Janabib Tribe in the Negev: Facts and Folkloric Traditions. *Notes on the Bedouin*, no .20: 9-21.

Bailey, Clinton, and Raphael Peled. 1975. *A Survey of the Bedouin Tribes in Sinai* (in Hebrew). Tel Aviv: Israel Ministry Defence.

Barker, Paul. 1981. Tent Schools of the Qashqai: A Paradox of Local Initiative and State Control. *Modern Iran: The Dialectics of Continuity and Change*, edited by M. E. Bonine and N. Keddie. Albany: State University of York Press.

Bar-Zvi, Sason. 1973. Governing Bedouin Tribes in the Negev. *Notes on the Bedouin*, no. 4: 26-32.

_____. 1977. *Bedouin tell about Beersheba* (in Hebrew). Beersheba: Ben-Gurion University of the Negev, Tuviaho Archives, Publication no.13: 1-33.

Bar-Zvi, Sason, 'Aref Abu-Rabi'a, and Gideon Kressel. 1998. *The Charm of Graves: Mourning Rituals and Tomb Worshipping Among the Negev Bedouin*. Tel Aviv: Israel Ministry Defence.

Berman, M. 1965. The Evolution of Beer-Sheva. *Annals of the American Geographic Association* 55: 315-16.

Bernstein-Tarrow, Norma. 1978. Education of the Bedouin Negev in the Context of Radical Socio-Economic Change. *Compare* 8, no.2: 141-47.

Bresslavsky, Joseph. 1946. *Do You Know the Country? The Negev* (in Hebrew). Tel-Aviv: Hakibutz Hameuchad.

Brewer, Douglas, and Emily Teeter. 1999. *Egypt and the Egyptians.* Cambridge: Cambridge University Press..

Burckhardt, John Lewis. 1822. *Travels in Syria and the Holy Land.* London: J. Murray.

Burckhardt. John Lewis. 1831. *Notes on the Bedouins Wahabys.* 2 vol. London: Colburn and R. Bentley.

Canaan, Tewfik. 1927. *Mohammedan Saints and Sanctuaries in Palestine.* Jerusalem: Ariel Publishing House.

Chatty, Dawn. 1978. Changing Sex Roles in Bedouin Society in Syria and Lebanon. *Women in the Muslim World*, edited by L. Beck and N. Keddie. Cambridge: Harvard University Press.

_____. 1990. The Current Stuation of the Bedouin in Syria, Jordan and Saudi Arabia and their prospects for the future. *Nomads in a Changing World*, edited by C. Zalzman and J. Galaty. Naples: Instituto Universitario Orientale.

Cohen, Amnon. 1989. *Economic Life in Ottoman Jerusalem.* Cambridge: Cambridge University Press.

Cole, Donald. 1975. *Nomads of the Nomads: The al-Murrah Bedouin of the Empty Quarter.* Chicago: Adline.

Cole, Donald and Soraya Altorki. 1998. *Bedouin, Settlers, and Holiday-Makers: Egypt's Changing Northwest Coast.* Cairo: The American University in Cairo Press.

Connan, Jacques, Arie Nissenbaum, and Daniel Dessort. 1992. Molecular archaeology: Export of Dead Sea asphalt to Canaan and Egypt in the Chalcolithic-Early Bronze Age (4th-3rd millennium B.C.). *Geochimica et Cosmochimica Acta* 56: 2743-59.

Cornfeld, Peretz. 1947. *Palestine Personalia.* Tel Aviv: Sefer Press.

al-Dabbagh, Mustafa. 1991. *Bildaduna Filastin* (in Arabic). Beirut: Dar al-Tali'a.

Danin, Ezra and Ya'acov Shimoni. 1981. *Documents and Portraits from the Arab Gangs Archives, in the Arab Revolt in Palestine (1936-39)* (in Hebrew). Jerusalem: The Magnes Press, The Hebrew University.

Dickson, Violet. 1955. *The Wild Flowers of Kuwait and Bahrain.* London: George Allen and Unwin.

Diqs, Isaak. 1984. *Bedouin Boyhood.* New York: Universe Books.

D.N.B.1931-1940=702-706,

D.N.B. 1941-1950=904-907, 930-932,

D.N.B. 1951-1960=206-207,

D.N.B. 1961-1970= 704-706, 918-922,

Doumani, Beshara. 1995. *Rediscovering Palestine. Merchants and Peasants in Jabal Nablus, 1700-1900.* Berkeley: University of California Press.

al-Eisa, Abdulaziz, A. 1985. *An Ecological Study of Bedouin Elementary School Education in Hail Province: Saudi Arabia*. Ph.D. dissertation, University of Arizona.

El-Eini, Rosa. 1999a. British Agricultural-Educational Institutions in Mandate Palestine and Their Impress on the Rural Landscape. *Middle Eastern Studies 35*, no.1: 98-114.

_____ 1999b. British Forestry Policy in Mandate Palestine, 1929-48: Aims and Realities. *Middle East Studies 35*, no.3: 72-155.

Encyc. Palest.III, 59-60, 545; V, 33. Encyc.Palest = *Encyclopaedia Palaestina* (Beirut: Encyclopaedia Palaestina Corporation), in Arabic.

Erskine, S. 1935. *Palestine of the Arabs*. London: Harrap.

Ettingon, Rami. 1979. The Period of the British Mandate, 1917-1948. *Beersheba Book* (in Hebrew), edited by Y. Gradus and E. Stern. Jerusalem: Keter Publishing House.

Evans-Pritchard, E., *The Sanusi of Cyrenaica*, Oxford: Oxford University Press, 1949.

Gal-Pe'er, I. 1979a. Beersheba and the Bedouin. *Beersheba Book* (in Hebrew), edited by Y. Gradus and E. Stern. Jerusalem: Keter Publishing House.

_____ 1979b. The Jewish Attendance in Beersheba before the establishment of Israel.*Beersheba Book*, edited by Y. Gradus and E. Stern.

_____ 1991a. *Beersheba Sights* (in Hebrew), edited by Gideon Biger and Ely Schiller. Jerusalem: Ariel.

_____ 1991b. The British Military Cemetery in Beersheba. *Beersheba Sights*.

Gavron, Daniel. 1965. Education for the Bedouin. *New Outlook 8*, no.6: 24-28.

Gerber, Haim. 1985. *Ottoman Rule in Jerusalem, 1890-1914*. Berlin: Klaus Schwarz Verlag.

al-Ghuri, Amil. 1972. *Filastin 'abra Sittina 'Aman*. Beirut: Dar al-Nahar li-Nashr.

Ginat, Joseph. 1984. Blood Revenge in Bedouin Society. The Changing Bedouin, edited by Emanuel Marx and Avshalom Shmueli. New Brunswick: Transaction Books.

_____. 2000. Blood Revenge, Outcasting Mediation, and Family Honor. (in Hebrew). Tel Aviv: Haifa University Press & Zmora-Bitan.

Gorham, A.B. 1978. *The Design and Management of Pastoral Development: The Provision of Education in Pastoral Areas*. London: Overseas Development Institute Report.

Government of Palestine 1946. Anglo-American Committee for inquiry, *A survey of Palestine*, 151, table 8b.

Government of Palestine 1947. *Department of Education, Statistical Tables and Diagrams, Scholastic Year 1944/45.*Jerusalem: Government Printing Office.

Government of Palestine 1935, 1938, 1944/45. Statistical Abstracts of Palestine. Jerusalem: Government Printing Office.

Government of Palestine 1946. *A Survey of Palestine* I: 150; 2: 638.

Government of Palestine 1937a. *Report of Palestine and Trans-Jordan.* London.

Government of Palestine 1937b. *Palestine Royal Commission, Peel Committee.*

Government of Palestine 1945/46. *Department of Education.* Jerusalem: Government Printing Office.

*Government of Palestine*1925-1948. *Department of Veterinary Services.* Jerusalem: Government Printing Office.

al-Haj, Majid. 1995. *Education, Empowerment and Control: The Case of the Arabs in Israel.* New York: State University of New York Press.

Havakook, Ya'acov. 1998. *Footprints in the Sand: The Bedouin Trackers of the Israel Army* (in Hebrew). Tel Aviv: Israel Ministry of Defence.

Hashkafa. 1908. Editorials, nos. 71, 72.

Heron, Pauline. 1983. Education for Nomads. *Nomadic Peoples*, no.13: 61-68.

Higgins, Rosalyn. 1969. *The Middle East*, vol. 1 of *United Nations Peace Keeping, 1946-1967, Documents and Commentary.* London: Oxford University Press.

Hourani, Albert. 1968. Ottoman Reform and the Politics of Notables. *The Beginnings of Modernization in the Middle East: The Nineteenth Century.* Edited by W. R. Polk and R. L. Chambers. Chicago: University of Chicago Press.

Hutchinson, Elmo. 1956. *Violent Truce.* New York: The Devin-Adair Company.

Israeli Defence Forces (IDF). 1954. *The Negev Bedouin.* Tel Aviv: Israeli Defence Forces Publisher.

Israel Ministry of Education. 1951. *Sefer ha-khinukh viha-Tarbut.* Jerusalem: Ministry of Education publisher.

Ismail [Ismael], F. M. 1976. *Al-Taghayyur wal-ttanmiyah fi al-mujtama' al-Sahrawi* (in Arabic). Alexandria: Alexandria University Press.

Jabbur, Jibrail. 1995. *The Bedouins and the Desert: Aspects of Nomadic Life in the Arab East.* Albany: State University of New York Press.

Jamali, Mohammed. 1934. *The New Iraq, Its Problem of Bedouin Education.* New York: Teachers College, Columbia University.

Jordan Museum of Popular Traditions. 1998. Amman.

Karni, Nurit. 1976. *The [Bedouin] Education System in Southern Sinai.* Final review and report submitted to the Department of Arab Education, Ministry of Education, Jerusalem.

Katakura, Motoko. 1977. *Bedouin Village: A Study of a Saudi Arabian People in Transition.* Tokyo: University of Tokyo Press.

Kay, Shirley. 1978. *The Bedouin.* New York: Crane, Russak and Company Inc.

Kennett, Austin. 1968. *Bedouin Justice: Law and Custom among the Egyptian Bedouin.* London: Frank Cass and Co.

Khogali, Mustafa. 1981. Sedentarization of the Nomads: Sudan. *The Future of Pastoral Peoples,* edited by J. G. Galaty et al. Ottawa: The International Development Centre.

Khoury,Philip, S. 1983. *Urban Notables and Arab Nationalism: The Politics of Damascus, 1860-1920.* Cambridge: Cambridge University Press.

Kressel, G. M., and J. Ben-David. 1995. The Bedouin Market-Corner Stone for the Founding of Beersheba: Bedouin Traditions about the Development of the Negev Capital in the Ottoman Period. *Nomadic Peoples* 36/37: 119-144.

Kushner, David. 1995. *A Governor in Jerusalem: The City and Province in the Eyes of Ali Ekrem Bey 1906-1908* (in Hebrew). Jerusalem: Yad Izhak Ben-Zvi.

_____ 1996. Ali Ekrem Bey, Governor of Jerusalem, 1906-1908. *International Journal of Middle East Study,* no. 28: 349-62.

Lancaster, W. 1981. *The Rawala Bedouin Today.* London: Cambridge University Press.

Layne, Linda. 1994. *Home and Home Land: The Dialogics of Tribal and National Identities in Jordan.* Princeton: Princeton University Press.

Lewis, Norman. 1987. *Nomads and Settlers in Syria and Jordan,* 1800-1980. Cambridge: Cambridge University Press.

Longrigg, Stephen. 1925. *Four Centuries of Modern Iraq.* Oxford: The Clarendon Press.

Luke, Harry Charles and Edward Keith-Roach. 1922. *The Handbook of Palestine.* London: Macmillan.

_____ 1930. *The Handbook of Palestine and Trans-Jordan.* London: Macmillan.

al-Maddy, Munib and Sulayman Musa. 1959. *Tarikh al-Urdon fi al-qarn al-'Ishrin.* Amman: Publishing rights reserved for the authors.

Mahjub, Muhammad. 1981. *Anthropolojia al-Mujtama'at al-Badawiya.* Al-Iskandariya: al-Hay'a al-'Ama lel-Kitab.

Maimon, David. 1975. The Bedouin Trackers. *Notes on the Bedouin*, no. 6: 42-50.

Ma'oz, Moshe, editor. 1975. *Studies on Palestine During the Ottoman Period*. The Magnes Press, The Hebrew University, Institute of Asian and African Studies. Jerusalem: Yad Izhak Ben-Zvi.

Mar'i, Sami. 1978. *Arab Education in Israel*. Syracuse, N.Y.: Syracuse University Press.

Marx, Emanuel. 1967. *Bedouin of the Negev*. Manchester: University of Manchester Press.

Marx, Emanuel, and M., Sela. 1980. The Situation of the Negev's Bedouin, Appendix No. 1. *Ben-Mayer's Team for Evacuation and Resettlement of the Bedouin*. Tel Aviv: TAHAL.

Me'ir, Avino'am. 1986. Pastoral Nomads and the Dialectics of Development and Modernization, Delivering Public Educational Services to the Israeli Negev Bedouin. *Environment and Planning Development: Society and Space* 4: 85-95.

———— 1997. *As Nomadism Ends*. Boulder: Westview Press.

Me'ir, Avino'am, and Dov Barnea. 1985. *The Development of the Negev Bedouin Educational System* (in Hebrew). Beersheba: Ben-Gurion University of the Negev, Department of Geography.

Midhat, Ali. 1973. *The Life of Midhat Pasha*. New York: Arno Press.

Miller, Naomi. 1996. Seed Eaters of the Ancient Near East: Human or Herbivore? *Current Anthropology* 37, no.3: 521-28.

Miller, Ylana. 1985. *Government and Society in Rural Palestine*, 1920-1948. Austin: University of Texas Press.

Mohammed, A. 1973. The Nomadic and the Sedentary: Polar Complementaries-Not Polar Opposites. *The Desert and the Sown*, edited by C. Nelson. Berkeley: University of California.

Mohammed, M. J. 1981. Planning Policy and Bedouin Society in Oman. *The Future of Pastoral Peoples*", edited by J. G. Galaty et al.

Morris, Benny. 1996. *Israel's Border Wars, 1949-1956* (in Hebrew). Tel Aviv: 'Am Oved.

Morris,Yaakov. 1961. *Masters of the Desert: 6,000 Years in the Negev*. New York: G. P. Putnam and Sons.

Muhsam, Helmut Victor. 1966. *Bedouin of the Negev: Eight Demographic Studies*. Jerusalem: Jerusalem Academic Press.

al-Musallam, Bassama Khalid. 1984. *Women's Education in Kuwait and Its Effect on Future Expectations: An Ethnography of a Girls' Sex-Segregated Secondary School*. Ph.D. dissertation, State University of New York.

Musil, Alois. 1928a. *The Manners and Customs of the Rwala Bedouins*. New York: American Geographical Society.

Musil, Alois. 1928b. *Northern Nejd*. New York: American Geographical Society.

Nesbitt, Mark. 1995. Plants and People in Ancient Anatolia. *Biblical Archaeologist* 58: 2.

al-Nimr, Ihsan. 1961. *Tarikh Jabal Nabulus wa-l-Balqa* (in Arabic). Nabulus: Matba'at Jam'iyat 'Ummal al-Matabe' al-Ta'awuniya.

Nissenbaum, Arie. 1978. Dead Sea Asphalt-Historical Aspects. *American Association of Petroleum Geologists* 62: 837-44.

Nkinyangi, John. 1981. Education for Nomadic Pastoralists: Development Planning by Trial and Error. *The Future of Pastoral People*, edited by J. Galaty, et al. Ottawa:The International Development Centre.

Palmer, E. H. 1871. *The Desert of the Exodus*. Vol. 2. Cambridge: Deighton, Bell.

Patai, Raphael. 1971. *Society, Culture and Change in the Middle East*. Philadelphia: University Pennsylvania Press.

Pink, Pinhas. 1991. Beersheba Conquest in the World War I. *Beersheba Sights,* edited by Gideon Biger and Ely Schiller. Jerusalem: Ariel.

Public Record Office (PRO FO) 371/5124/149, letter dated 26 November 1920.

Qubain, Fahim. 1966. *Education and Science in the Arab World*. Baltimore: The Johns Hopkins Press.

Quran 57: 22-23.

Rogan, Eugene. 1996. Asiret Mektebi: Abdulhamid II's School for Tribes (1892-1907). *International Journal of Middle East Study* 28: 83-107.

Sadat, Deena, R. 1970. *Urban Notables in the Ottoman Empire*. Ph.D. dissertation, Rutgers: The State University [University Microfilms, Inc., Ann Arbor, Michigan, 1970 [1969].

Saleh, Mohsen. 1996. *Military and Police Forces in Palestine 1917-1939* (in Arabic). Amman: Dar al-Nafa'es.

Shahshahani, Soheila. 1995. Tribal Schools of Iran: Sedentarization through Education. *Nomadic Peoples*, no. 36/37: 145-55.

Shamir, Shimon. 1965. *A Modern History of the Arabs in the Middle East* (in Hebrew). Tel Aviv: Reshafim.

Sharon, Moshe. 1964. The Bedouin in Israel during the 18th and 19th Centuries. Master's thesis, Jerusalem: The Hebrew University, Department of Islamic Studies.

_____. 1975. The Political Role of the Bedouin in Palestine in the Sixteenth and Seventeenth Centuries. *Studies on Palestine During the Ottoman Period*, edited by Moshe Ma'oz. The Magnes Press, The Hebrew University, Institute of Asian and African Studies. Jerusalem: Yad Izhak Ben-Zvi.

Shavit,Yaacov, Yaacov Foldstein, and Haim Be'er, editors. 1983. *Personalities in Eretz-Israel 1799-1948, A Biographical Dictionary* (in Hebrew). Tel Aviv: 'Am Oved.

Shimoni, Yacob. 1947. *The Arabs of Palestine*. TelA.viv: 'Am Oved.

Shuqayr, Na'um. 1916. *Tarikh Sina al-Qadim wal-Hadith wa-Geghrafiatha*. Cairo: Matba'at al-Ma'aref.

Sorek, Chagit, and Etan Ayalon, editors. 1993. *Colors from Nature, Natural Colors in Ancient Times* (in Hebrew). Tel Aviv: Eretz Israel Museum.

Stewart, Frank. H. 1986. *Bedouin Boundaries in Central Sinai and the Southern Negev: A Document from the Ahaywat Tribe*. Wiesbaden: O. Harrassowitz.

Szyliowicz, Joseph, S. 1973. *Education and Modernization in the Middle East*. Ithaca: Cornell University Press.

Tal, Hilla. 1991. Beersheba during British Mandate. *Beersheba Sights*, edited by Gideon Biger and Ely Schiller. Jerusalem: Ariel.

Tibawi, Abd al-Latif. 1956. *Arab education in Mandatory Palestine: A Study of Three Decades of British Administration*. London: Luzac and Company.

Wasserstein, Bernard. 1991. *The British in Palestine: The Mandatory Government and the Arab-Jewish Conflict 1917-1929*, second edition. Cambridge: Basil Blackwell.

Weitz, Joseph. 1947. *Our Settlement Activities in a Period of Storm and Stress 1936-1947* (in Hebrew). Jerusalem: Sifriat Poalim.

Yousuf, Abd el-Kader. 1956. *The British educational policy in the Arab public schools of Palestine during the Mandatory period*. Ph.D. dissertation, Indiana University.

Zbida, Aharon. 1975. *The Bedouin Education in Southern Sinai*. Report submitted to the Department of Education, Southern Sinai.

Ze'evi, Dror. 1996. *An Ottoman Century: The District of Jerusalem in the 1600s*. New York: State University of New York.

Index

General